"Wow, this book is packed full of so much helpful information and tasks. It really helped me with managing my portfolio."

- Lee Rouse
Owner & Founder of
LMR Consulting Limited

"What a massive insight into the day-to-day requirements of asbestos management. I now feel totally comfortable in advising my clients with what they need to do to stay on the right side of compliance."

- Daniel Wicks
Managing Director of
Wicks Controls Services Ltd.

ASBESTOS
THE DARK ARTS

The dutyholder's shortcut to asbestos knowledge, understanding requirements and keeping people safe without overspending, wasting time or going it alone

Ian Stone & Neil Munro

Don't Forget To Download
The #BONUS Materials For Free!

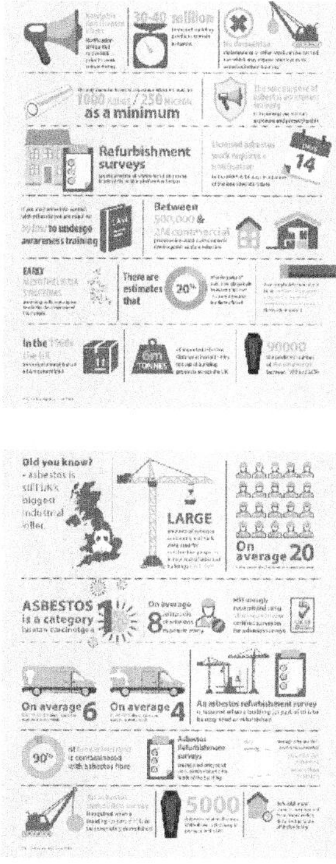

All you have to do is go here:

www.asbestosthedarkarts.com/bonus-fact-sheets

LEGAL NOTICES

The information presented herein represents the view of the authors as of the date of publication. Because of the rate with which conditions change, the authors reserve the right to alter and update their opinion based on the new conditions.

This book is for informational purposes only. While every attempt has been made to verify the information provided in this book, neither the authors nor their affiliates/partners assume any responsibility for errors, inaccuracies or omissions.

Any slights of people or organisations are unintentional. If advice concerning legal, financial or any other real estate related matters is needed, the services of a fully qualified professional should be sought. This book is not intended for use as a source of legal or accounting advice.

Information from HSE guidance documentation have been utilised in areas either as reference or have been directly reproduced. The documentation can be obtained from the HSE website: www.hse.gov.uk/asbestos.

Asbestos
The Dark Arts

The dutyholder's shortcut to asbestos knowledge, understanding requirements and keeping people safe without overspending, wasting time or going it alone

Ian Stone & Neil Munro

This book is packed with **facts, pointers and tasks** to help you understand all the parts of asbestos management.

Learn about how many **millions of tonnes** of asbestos the UK has imported and used over the years.

Find out the **easy way to select** asbestos surveyors and contractors.

Discover how you can keep people safe and manage asbestos by following **6 simple principles**.

Table of Contents

INTRODUCTION

Warning!

Asbestos Kills!

Asbestos kills. It kills a lot of people in the UK and all over the world.

This book has been written from the two authors' perspective as professional asbestos consultants with a view of cutting through all of the complicated elements that surround asbestos and its management.

The chapters are packed to the brim with information and asbestos knowledge gleaned from over 30 years collectively as asbestos consultants in the UK.

The book can be used as a quick reference guide to quickly help you bring your asbestos management in line.
For those that want the quick answers, each chapter has a bullet point section, which summarises the chapter's message.

For those that not only want to ensure asbestos compliance, but also want to genuinely educate themselves further, there's lots of information laced throughout this book.

#BONUS ITEMS = Getting Stuff Done

Additionally, as well as all of the information, there are several "Getting Stuff Done" tasks and exercises throughout. These will help you understand your asbestos situation and where you are with compliance.

There are various sections within this book that suggest the use of consultancies and contractors over a DIY approach.

It would be easy to say it's for the generation of work for the authors' businesses. However, it's simply not the case. These opinions have been formed from a combined experience of 30+ years in the asbestos industry. The information and opinions come from a background of always providing impartial and independent advice. The idea of this book is to cut through a lot of the over complicated elements that surround asbestos, not to become an overnight expert in every aspect.

There are elements that cannot be simplified and made easy and elements that require certain things to achieve them such as accreditations and licences.

This is where consultants and contractors always come in. This book will help you achieve getting the right people on board, so you have an **Asbestos Power Team** behind you to assist you with your asbestos management.

It's the dutyholder's job to have enough knowledge and competency to manage these external contractors to ensure they are working fully in line with your asbestos management goals.

Ian and Neil have picked up the pieces so many times. That's why it's important to get help for any of the areas you are unsure of or not fully competent in.

Get the right team on board and use them to their fullest to ensure your asbestos management is bulletproof, so that you can rest assured your time and money is spent wisely keeping people safe.

If you're still unsure about any element of your asbestos management, there is a section at the back of the book whereby you can contact us for a complimentary asbestos audit.

You now have everything in your power to step forward and proactively manage your asbestos, but if you want help in removing your asbestos headache, we're also here to help you further.

PREFACE

What can you expect?

What's in the book?

Remember that TV advert that said *"Tax doesn't have to be Taxing"*? We all know the kicker to that advert is that tax is bloody taxing unless you're an accountant!

Thankfully, asbestos isn't tax, but it is bloody complicated – we're not going to lie to you!
Trying to decipher the reams and reams of regulations, approved codes of practice and guidance is a mammoth task for anyone.

That's how we've made our careers out of working in this niche industry, gaining knowledge, understanding the intricacies and helping clients manage their asbestos.

Up until now, all you've really had to go on are the documents mentioned above. They're hard work for anyone… think of *War and Peace* but not as interesting a story to keep you motivated.

This is where we (Ian and Neil) have stepped in with this book. It simply cuts to the chase and avoids the bollox concerning all areas in and around asbestos management.

We've worked together for over 16 years, being great friends, business partners and ultimately asbestos geeks. We joined forces to write this book to make your life easier.

Wherever we can, we've simplified the overcomplicated information that surrounds asbestos management, allowing you to make the decisions you need to be more informed and more quickly.

The book's main aim is to help people and businesses understand asbestos and to ultimately stop people getting exposed to the hidden killer.

CHAPTER 1

What is asbestos?

The background science bit!

Asbestos is a mineral that is formed in rock. That's right – it comes straight out of the ground and is mined.

It doesn't grow! It doesn't appear! It doesn't produce noxious gas! It's not man-made!

Asbestos is a mineral that is mined in similar fashion to other items that have more commonly been mined e.g., coal, talc and gold.

It is a silicate mineral, a chain silicate to be precise. Silicates are the earth's most common mineral types.

The main places asbestos was mined commercially were Brazil, Canada, China, India, Kazakhstan, Russia and South Africa.

Once the rock was broken off into manageable pieces, it was then usually milled on site by breaking the rock down to break out the useful raw asbestos fibres.

Chrysotile (White) Asbestos Rock

How many asbestos types are there?

There are six types of asbestos, of which three were extensively used on a commercial scale.

We'll call them **"The Big 3"**.

The other types, we'll call "The Minor 3", were used, but in far lower quantities and never on the same commercial scale as "The Big 3". "The Minor 3" were used on a small scale and were often found in asbestos materials as by-products from mining "The Big 3".

"The Big 3" types:

- Chrysotile *(cry-so-tile)*
- Amosite *(amo-site)*/Grunerite *(grun-er-rite)*
- Crocidolite *(cro-sid-o-lite)*

Now as you can see, these names don't exactly roll off the tongue. So, the industry gave them easier to remember (and say) names. These names were based on the raw colour of the asbestos fibre.

Out of The Big 3, there was a giant. Chrysotile white asbestos was the most commonly used asbestos. In fact, approximately **90% of all asbestos-containing materials in the UK contain Chrysotile White Asbestos.**

Chrysotile = White Asbestos

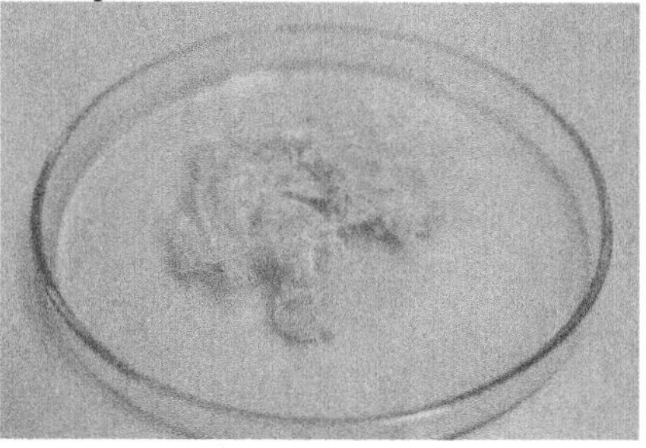

Amosite = Brown Asbestos

Crocidolite = Blue Asbestos

"The Minor 3" types:

- Fibrous Tremolite *(Trem-o-lite)*
- Fibrous Actinolite *(Act-in-o-lite)*
- Fibrous Anthophyllite *(An-tho-phy-llite)*

The Minor 3 were never given common names due to their lesser usage.

Fibrous Tremolite

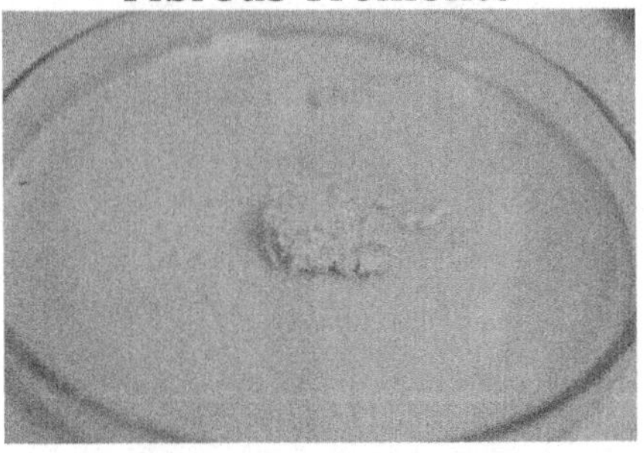

Fibrous Actinolite

Fibrous Anthophyllite

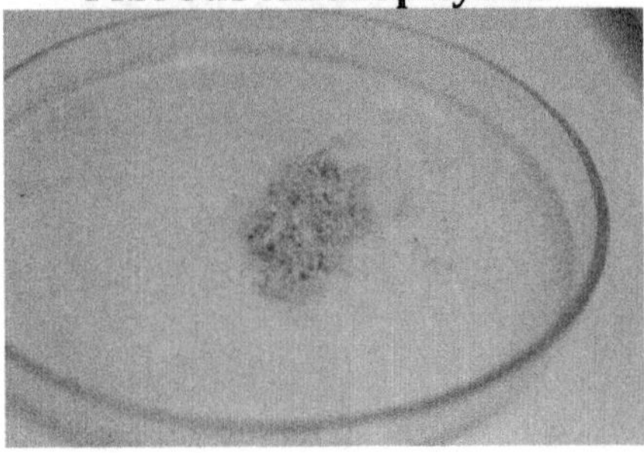

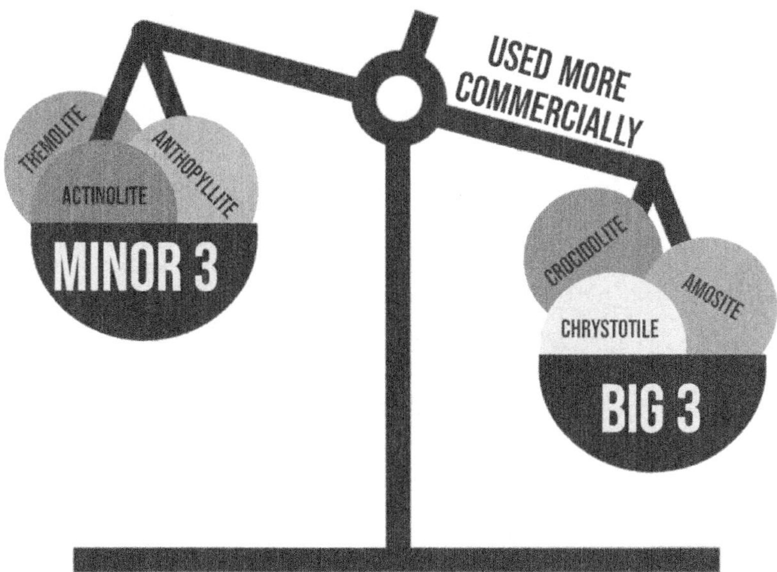

If you want to impress (or bore!) your friends down at the pub, you can tell them that although there are six recognised asbestos types, there are actually two Chrysotiles!

One was mined in South Africa and one was mined in Canada. They are both essentially the same but give slightly different colour changes under the microscope.

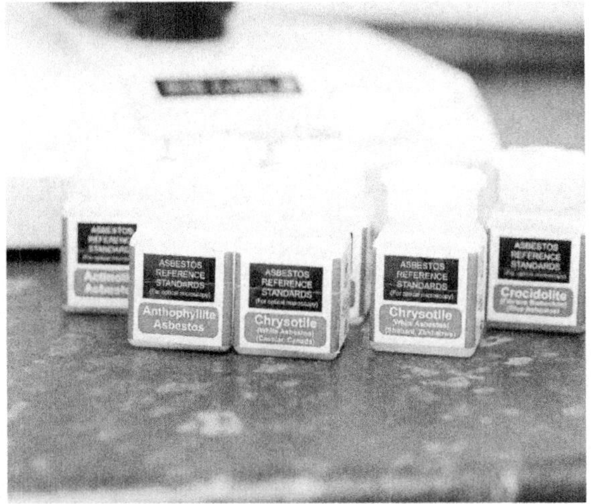

Another fact – you may be wondering why Amosite has two names? Well, Amosite got its name as an acronym of **A**sbestos **M**ines **o**f **S**outh Africa where it was first mined, and the name was mixed with its mineral name Gruner**ite** giving the name Amosite.

Only Grunerite from South Africa is called Amosite. Grunerite mined anywhere else in the world is just called Grunerite.

Are all asbestos types the same?

Each type of asbestos falls into one of two mineral groups of Serpentine or Amphibole:

Serpentine

Chrysotile

Amphibole

Amosite (Grunerite)
Crocidolite
Anthophyllite
Actinolite
Tremolite

These two categories of minerals relate to the fibre types and basic characteristics they hold.

Serpentine fibres (just Chrysotile) are a wavy/curly fibre.

Amphibole fibres (all other fibres) are straight and needle-like fibres.

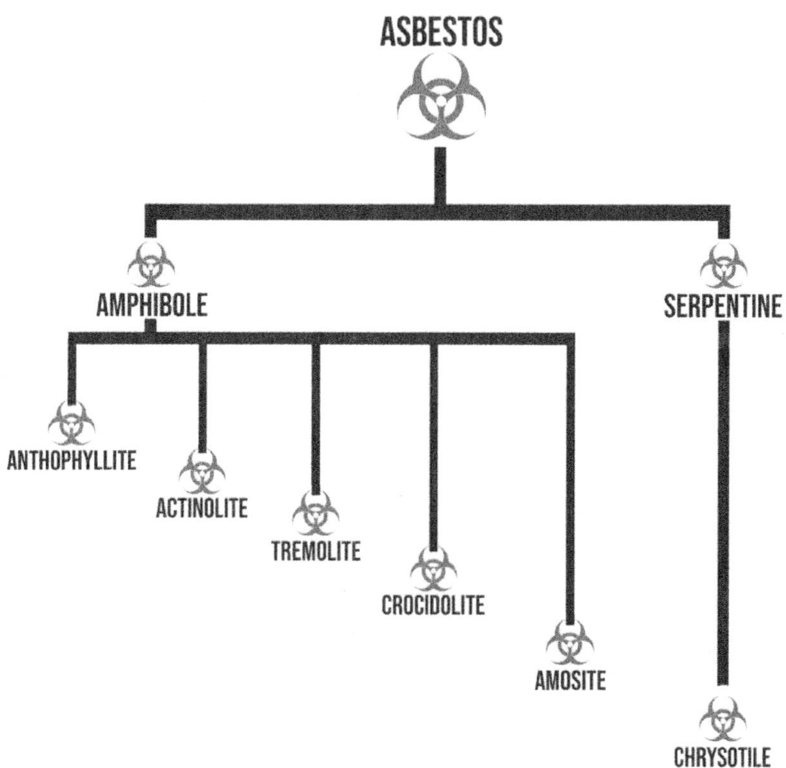

What are asbestos fibres like?

Sample Analysis

Serpentine (Chrysotile) fibres have great tensile strength, are silky in appearance and are very flexible. However, they are inelastic. These properties mean that it could be spun and woven.

Amphibole (all other fibres) have great tensile strength and are elastic.

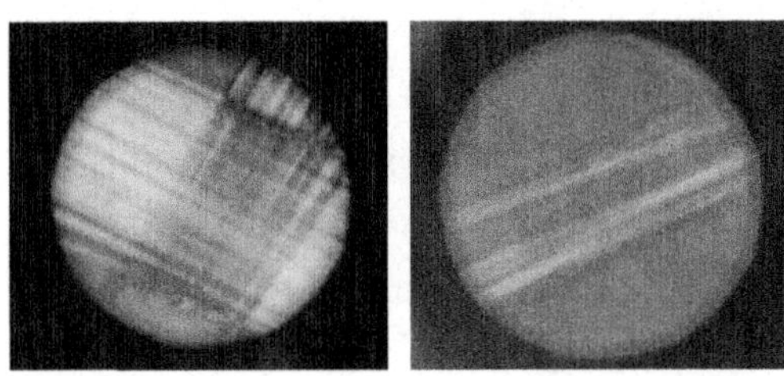

Asbestos Fibres Under Polarized Light

Why do you need to know this? Well, understanding the basic characteristics of the different asbestos types will help you understand why they were used. We'll go into more detail further in the book.

CHAPTER BULLET POINTS

- Asbestos comes from rocks.
- Asbestos is a mineral.
- Asbestos is a chain silicate mineral.
- There are six types of asbestos fibre.
- Three types (The Big 3) were commercially mined more.
- Asbestos is split into two groups – Serpentine and Amphibole.

CHAPTER 2

Why was asbestos used?

What's so great about it?

Speak to any industrial chemist (as you would) and they will tell you that asbestos really is a magical mineral.

Before you read this next section, clear your mind of all the negative thoughts you may have about asbestos. We want you to do this so you can truly appreciate why this material was used!

So, what's so special about these minerals?

Incredible Heat Resistance

Asbestos has an incredible resistance to heat. It does not burn or melt until it gets to an extremely high temperature, somewhere around 1,500°C. That's more than plaster, more than fibreglass and even more than steel.

Ultimate Insulator

It is an excellent insulator and does not easily allow heat, electricity, light or sound to pass through it.

Super Strong

Asbestos is super strong and has a tensile strength that surpasses steel.

Insoluble in water

Asbestos is insoluble in water, which means it can't be dissolved in water.

Immense Chemical Resistance

Asbestos can resist the destructive effects of powerful acids and alkalines.

Tasteless

Asbestos has no detectable aroma or taste.

Flexible

Asbestos is flexible, meaning it can bend easily without breaking. It can be spun and woven to make items like textiles, ropes and woven products.
So, there you have it. Sounds amazing, doesn't it?

It's a material that has so many useful properties and is top of the class in almost all areas. To top it off, these materials were NOT MAN-MADE. They're a naturally abundant resource mined from the ground.

There's just one more reason, and probably the most important reason, to why asbestos was used, Cost = asbestos was **CHEAP!**

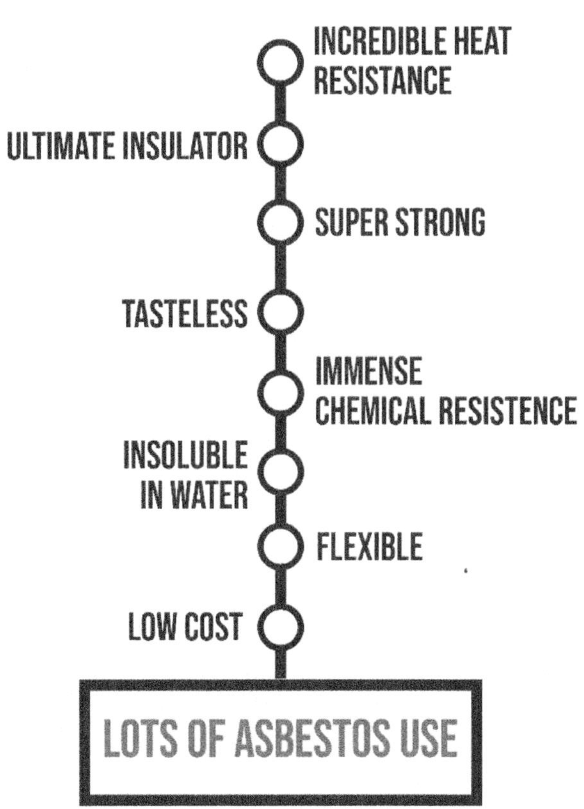
INCREDIBLE HEAT RESISTANCE
ULTIMATE INSULATOR
SUPER STRONG
TASTELESS
IMMENSE CHEMICAL RESISTENCE
INSOLUBLE IN WATER
FLEXIBLE
LOW COST
LOTS OF ASBESTOS USE

Prior to the boom years of asbestos use, asbestos was used in low quantities, as it was hard to source. This was prior to the advancement of mining techniques.

As the mining process advanced, suddenly asbestos was available in abundance. And it was like a gold rush. Mining companies sprung up across the world in a race to be the greatest producers.

Here's where the UK took dominance. Although asbestos has never been commercially mined in the UK, we used it in manufacturing.
In fact, we were home to one of the world's largest producers and manufacturers of asbestos-containing products. Turner and Newall, originally located in Rochdale and Manchester, was one of the top companies in the UK and only completely ceased world operations in 2001.

CHAPTER BULLET POINTS

- Asbestos has incredible heat resistance.
- Asbestos is an excellent insulator.
- Asbestos is super strong.
- Asbestos is insoluble in water.
- Asbestos has immense chemical resistance.
- Asbestos has no detectable aroma or taste.
- Asbestos was cheap.

CHAPTER 3

Where was asbestos used?

What uses does it have?

Put simply, EVERYWHERE! In fact, it would have been easier to call this chapter "where wasn't asbestos used", although that would have been a disappointingly short chapter.

As we've already said, asbestos was used everywhere. In this chapter, we want to show you where the most common uses are but also tell you about some unusual ones.

Before we get into that, there are a couple of core factors you need to know about in order to understand what makes one asbestos product more dangerous than the next.

The two core factors are:

- **Density of Material**
- **Amount of Asbestos Content**

Low density (soft) materials with a **high asbestos content** have a high risk of releasing asbestos fibre if disturbed.

High density (hard) materials with **low asbestos content** have a lower risk of releasing asbestos fibre if disturbed.

Other factors apply when evaluating each asbestos material's risk. These include the condition of the material and its surface treatment. This forms the basis of a material risk assessment, which will be explained further in Chapter 10.

Why do you need to know this?

Understanding the risk from the asbestos material is essential in determining how you will manage the material and prevent people from being exposed to it.

Loose Insulation

Loose fill insulation to ceiling void

What Is It?:
Pure 100% loose asbestos fibre

Density of Material:
Low density - Very soft material

Amount of Asbestos Content:
High asbestos content - 100%
Mainly Crocidolite and Chrysotile used

Where it was Used:
Loose asbestos insulation or "loose fill asbestos" is now very rare to find. This is simply down to the hazard it poses and most of it has been removed.

It was used to insulate lofts, placed as fire packing around cables and insulation between floors. Paper bags or paper sacks were filled with loose insulation, which were used for sound insulation between floors or walls.

Sprayed Coating

Sprayed coating ceiling

What Is It?:
Asbestos fibre mixed with a Portland cement binder, which was spray applied onto surfaces.

Density of Material:
Low density – Very soft material

Amount of Asbestos Content:
High asbestos content – 55% - 85%
All asbestos types used but mainly Crocidolite and Amosite

Where it was Used:
Sprayed coatings were used as thermal and anti-condensation insulation on the underside of roofs and sometimes the sides of industrial buildings and warehouses.

It was used as acoustic insulation in theatres and halls, as fire protection on steel and reinforced concrete beams/columns and on the underside of floors.

The spraying of this material on application made it go everywhere. For example, if a beam was intentionally sprayed, the sprayed coating wouldn't be just on the beam, it would be on the ceiling, walls, floors and anything else in between. This often gets overlooked when trying to manage this material.

Thermal Insulation

Asbestos pipe insulation

What Is It?:
This material type covers many variants and is classified as any material that was used to provide thermal insulation to an item. A hand applied/mixed insulation, which was applied to pipes and boilers.

Preformed insulation sections (similar in appearance to the modern fibreglass insulation sections) referred to in the industry as "Sectional".

There were preformed insulation blocks, corrugated paper (used on pipes), ropes, quilts and blankets.

Density of Material:
Generally low density – Soft materials

Amount of Asbestos Content:
Generally high asbestos content – 6 - 85% (Mostly on the higher side)

Where it was Used:
Mostly to insulate pipes, boilers, calorifiers, tanks, pressure vessels. Used in all types of properties ranging from factories, hospitals and warehouses down to domestic houses.

Insulating Board

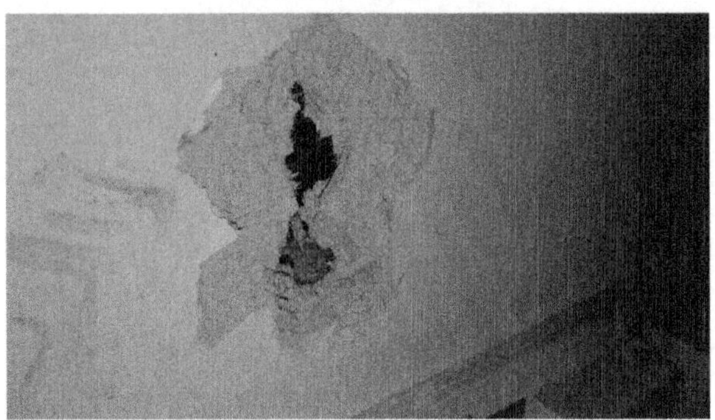

Asbestos insulating board

What Is It?:
Asbestos fibre mixed with calcium silicate

Density of Material:
Low density – Soft material

Amount of Asbestos Content:
High asbestos content – 15 - 40%

All types of asbestos used. Crocidolite was used in early boards. Amosite was extensively used on its own or with a mix of Chrysotile.

Where it was Used:
This material was used everywhere and was a key product for providing fire stop protection.

It was used as ceiling board/ceiling tiles, walls, infill panels, firebreaks, fire door backing panels, roofs, boxings, risers, linings, soffits, canopies, packers, linings to safes/filing cabinets, boiler casings... to name just a few.

Millboard

Asbestos millboard panels

What Is It?:
Asbestos fibre mixed with a matrix of clay and starch.

Density of Material:
Low density – Soft material

Amount of Asbestos Content:
High asbestos content – 37 - 97%
Crocidolite used for early boards. Mostly contained Chrysotile.

Where it was Used:
This material was used for general heat insulation and fire protection. Also used for insulation of electrical equipment and plants such as blow heaters.

Asbestos Paper & Cardboard

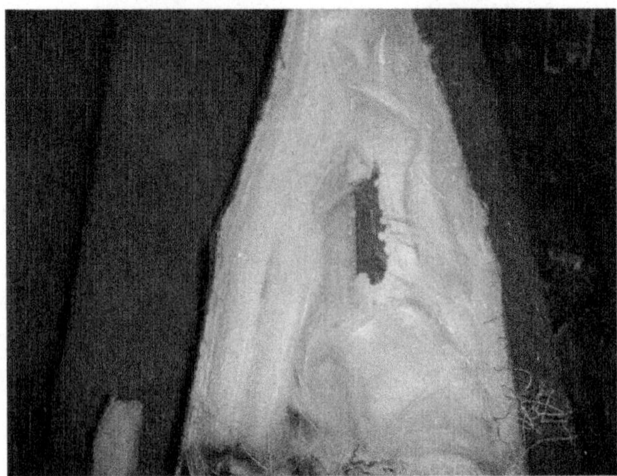

Paper lining below non-asbestos insulation

What Is It?:
Asbestos fibre down with water then compressed to form sheets of asbestos paper.

Density of Material:
Low density – Soft material

Amount of Asbestos Content:
High asbestos content – mostly 100%
Chrysotile asbestos used

Where it was Used:
Asbestos paper was generally used to line secondary materials. It was used to insulate electrical and heat equipment. It was used below fibreglass insulation on pipes, backing to floor covering, lining to combustible materials, such as fibreboard, below roof linings, etc.

Textiles, Ropes & Strings

Asbestos rope

What Is It?:
Asbestos fibre spun and woven.

Density of Material:
Low density - Soft material

Amount of Asbestos Content:
High asbestos content - 100%

Where it was Used:
Woven materials were used to create ropes and strings, which had many uses. Rope gaskets to boilers, skylights, safes, caulking in brickwork and jointing. Cloths were used to insulate boilers, pipes, exhausts, curtains, gloves, aprons and clothing.

Gaskets

Compressed asbestos fibre gasket (CAF Gasket)

What Is It?:
Asbestos fibre mixed with secondary materials and compressed.

Density of Material:
Generally low density – Soft Material

Amount of Asbestos Content:
High asbestos content – up to 90%
Mostly always Chrysotile used. Some Crocidolite used.

Where it was Used:
Gaskets have been used on a wide variety of boilers, heating systems and tanks including domestic, commercial and industrial. Gaskets have been used on machinery, appliances and products extensively. Some gasket materials continued to be used after asbestos prohibition in 1999 (through exemption).

Friction Products

Cement break shoes to lift motor

What Is It?:
Asbestos fibre bound within either resin or rubber.

Density of Material:
Generally high density – Hard material

Amount of Asbestos Content:
High asbestos content – 30 - 70%
Chrysotile used

Where it was Used:
Resin-based materials were used as brake and clutch shoes, pads or plates on transport vehicles, machinery and lifts.

Rubber-based materials were used as drive belts or conveyor belts on engines and conveyors.

Cement Products

Cement roof sheets

What Is It?:
Asbestos fibre mixed with cement

Density of Material:
High density – Hard material

Amount of Asbestos Content:
Low asbestos content. Mostly 10 - 25%. Some were as little as 4%. Industrial applications up to 50%.

Where it was Used:
Asbestos cement was extensively used and there were many applications of it. Profile sheets for roofing wall cladding, shuttering, etc. Compressed sheets, panels, tiles, slates, boards. Preform/moulded products included pipes, cisterns, tanks, drains, gutters, windowsills, bath panels. Draining board extractor hoods, coping and promenade tiles.

Composite Materials (Self-Sealed/Encapsulated Materials)

What Are They?
Asbestos fibre bonded with secondary material

Density of Material:
High density – Hard materials

Amount of Asbestos Content:
Generally low asbestos content – 1 - 50%
All types of asbestos have been used but mainly Chrysotile.

Where it was Used:

Textured coatings

Textured decorative coating to ceiling

3 - 5% Chrysotile asbestos mixed

Bitumen products

Damp proof course

Usually 8% chrysotile. Used as roofing felts, gutter linings and flashings, damp proofing, coatings of metals.

Flooring

Vinyl tiles and stair nosing

Thermoplastic floor tiles up to 25% asbestos. PVC vinyl floor tiles. PVC flooring normally 7% Chrysotile. Asbestos-backed PVC floors with a paper backing, paper 100% Chrysotile. Used on all types of floors.

Reinforced plastic and resin composites

Resin windowsills

1 - 10%. All types of asbestos used. Used for toilet cisterns, seats, window seals.

Asbestos Image Library

To view further asbestos images of the various different materials and locations they can be found within visit our website:

www.asbestosthedarkarts.com/asbestos-image-library

A really important question!

When was asbestos banned?

Asbestos was finally banned in the UK in **1999** – yes, as late as 1999!

What else happened in 1999?

Music

- *King of My Castle* by The Wamdue Project was #1 in the UK charts in November.
- The Red Hot Chilli Peppers released their *Californication* album.
- The Stereophonics released their *Performance and Cocktails* album.

Films in 1999

- *Toy Story 2* was released by Disney/Pixar.
- *The Matrix* starring Keanu Reeves and Laurence Fishburne was released.
- *Fight Club* starring Brad Pitt, Edward Norton and Helena Bonham Carter was released.

Technology in 1999

- Nokia's 3210 mobile phone was released, which went on to be one of the most successful and popular phones ever.
- The first USB flash drives were developed.
- The first Wiki was introduced with WikiWikiWeb.

Asbestos Prohibitions

There were other bans to this previously for the various types, but this was the final cut off point for all asbestos use in the UK.

Therefore, any building essentially constructed before this date may contain asbestos-containing materials. This is why we have such a huge problem with the stuff – it was used for decades in construction and manufacturing.

Word of warning!

Be careful whenever buying items online through auction sites that are made and shipped from places that still use asbestos! Although illegal, there are items on major auction sites for sale that are being sold as containing asbestos.

Heatproof gloves are the latest in a long line of items being manufactured in the Far East that are available online. We've also seen flasks, which contained asbestos pads on the inside lining of the glass, as well as various other items including BBQs.

This is the problem sometimes with international trade, whereby we deal with other countries that do not subscribe to our laws and rules.

If you would like to see more photos and examples of these materials, go to:

CHAPTER 4

What's the big problem?

The cold hard facts.

Asbestos kills – that is the long and short of it, that is what the big problem is. If you learn nothing else from this book, please, please, please, take this on board.

Asbestos kills and it is a very real and ongoing problem we face, which is going to be here for some time to come.

How many people die from asbestos?

As of 2018 in the UK, it is responsible for over 5,000 deaths per year. Let us write that again… **FIVE THOUSAND PEOPLE** each year are dying from exposure to asbestos.

Put that into perspective:

Five thousand is more than double the amount of people that die from road traffic accidents in the UK. That's right, more people die from asbestos than RTAs.
Five thousand is just under the amount that Accrington Stanley Football club stadium holds.

Can you imagine a football club-sized stadium of people dying each year due to a few fibres? That is what is happening right here in the UK.

In fact, exposure to asbestos is the UK's biggest industrial killer!

What makes this situation worse is that most exposure to asbestos comes from or is encountered in the workplace. Would you knowingly put yourself at risk for a job?

Why is asbestos hazardous?

One of the unique characteristics of asbestos is that it splits along its length. If you held a handful of asbestos, you would see the individual fibres with your naked eyes.

If you crushed the fibres in your hand, you would see the fibres split and become smaller. What you wouldn't see is that there would be millions of microscopic fibres split off from the original fibre bundles.

Fibres at microscopic level are thinner than human hairs.

When asbestos becomes this small and light, it can become airborne. Once airborne, it can remain suspended in the air for long periods of time.

Airborne asbestos can then be breathed in by humans. Some fibres will naturally be expelled by the body. However, some may lodge deep within the lungs.

Due to the characteristics of asbestos, such as resistance to chemical attack, the body's defences cannot deal with the asbestos fibres. Because they are not broken down by the body, they can stay for many years and work their way to the outer surface of the lungs.

Now there is no known safe level of asbestos exposure, but what we do know is that the greater amount of asbestos we're exposed to, the greater the risk of developing an asbestos-related disease.

Therefore, we need to make sure asbestos exposure is reduced as much as possible:

REDUCE ASBESTOS EXPOSURE = REDUCE RISK OF ASBESTOS DISEASE

So, you're probably thinking, REDUCE? Surely, there should be ZERO exposure to asbestos?

Well, we would agree, but this is simply impossible. Firstly, asbestos is a natural mineral and in the atmosphere already, but more importantly, asbestos was used everywhere.

In most towns and cities, you're never more than 50 meters from an asbestos product.

It was probably in the hospital you were born in, probably in the schools you went to, in the library, in your shopping centre, your office, your church, along your commute journey, and even in your home.

Why is asbestos killing so many people?

The issue is that we have a hell of a lot of asbestos in our buildings in the UK – we simply loved the stuff. We were the **BIGGEST USER** of Amosite Brown asbestos **in the world**. It's estimated that we imported between **5 & 6 MILLION TONNES** of raw fibre.

Put that into perspective:

- The average car weighs 2 tonnes.
  6 million tonnes = 3 million cars

- The Statue of Liberty weighs 225 tonnes.
  6 million tonnes = More than 26,000 Statues of Liberty

- The Shard weighs 12,500 tonnes.
  6 million tonnes = 480 Shards

- The HMS Queen Elizabeth, which is the UK's largest aircraft carrier, weighs 65,000 tonnes
  6 million tonnes = More than 92 HMS Queen Elizabeths.

We are talking big numbers and an almost incomprehensible amount of material imported into the UK. These 5 - 6 million tonnes of raw asbestos fibre were added to millions of tonnes of manufactured products.

During the height of asbestos use, if there was a product that was thought to be improved or made cheaper by adding asbestos, then it generally was.

This led to the huge usage of asbestos-containing materials being used across the entire country during construction and subsequent refurbishments.

As well as the moral obligation we have to stop people being exposed to asbestos, there are also Regulatory requirements that must be complied with.

Failing to comply with these can bring huge fines from the Health and Safety Executive or even prison sentences.

As well as the monetary impact, there are also commercial impacts that cannot be costed for because people's buying power is greatly affected by the press.

Ask yourself this one question – if you heard that the shop where you buy your lunch from was fined for not managing its asbestos properly, would you be straight in there the next day to buy your egg salad sandwich for lunch?

CHAPTER BULLET POINTS

- Asbestos kills.
- It's an issue worldwide but is massive in the UK.
- Over 5,000 people in the UK are dying each year.
- Deaths are due to exposure to asbestos.
- The body's defences cannot deal with the microscopic fibres.
- As well as morally, there is a requirement under regulation to ensure compliance.
- Non-compliance can bring court cases via HSE, which can result in massive fines or even prison time.
- Non-compliance can have a detrimental effect on people's health and also the PR of your business.

CHAPTER 5

What asbestos diseases are there?

Do all the diseases kill?

Now this really isn't a cheery subject. However, what we are going to talk about in this chapter is the very reason for writing this book.

It's the reason why asbestos is banned, why asbestos regulations are in place and why you should do everything in your power to protect yourself from this material.

Whenever we talk to new people about asbestos, the one thing they always say is, "Asbestos, that causes asbestosis, doesn't it?"

This is true but sadly, it isn't the greatest risk posed by exposure to asbestos.

What are the main asbestos diseases?

There are five main asbestos diseases:

- Pleural Plaques
- Diffuse Pleural Thickening
- Asbestosis
- Asbestos-related Lung Cancer
- Mesothelioma *(me-so-thee-lee-o-ma)*

The first thing you need to understand about asbestos diseases is that they are not instant. From being exposed to asbestos, there can be years before any signs of disease. This is referred to in medical terms as the latency.

**LATENCY =
TIME FROM FIRST EXPOSURE
TO WHEN DISEASE DEVELOPS**

The standard statement around diseases developing in a patient range from 15 to 50 years. However, over the years there have been several cases that appear to fall outside this range and could be fewer and more e.g., 5 to 50+ years.

We feel that this is one of the main reasons why some tradespeople don't take asbestos exposure very seriously. As there's no instant negative health effect from the exposure, they dismiss it as...

"Asbestos, what a load of bollocks."

"I've been working with this for years, there's nothing wrong with me!"
"Just a license to print money."

Even Donald Trump called asbestos poisoning a mob-led conspiracy!

Sadly, the evidence is stacked against them.

This is when we roll out these facts...

In the UK, on average

20 tradesmen die per week from asbestos exposure.

That includes...

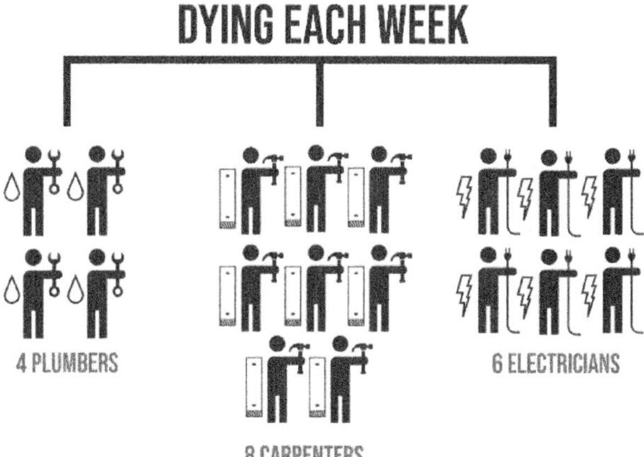

These are facts, and this really isn't a load of bollocks as some people proclaim!

Pleural Plaques

Pleural plaques are areas of pleural thickening. Simply put, this is the thickening of sections of the lining that surrounds the lung. The areas of thickening are usually well defined in areas. They are formed on the lining on the chest wall and are tough sinewy (tough fibrous tissue) in nature.

They are caused as the asbestos fibres lodge and then work their way into the outer lining of the lung. They then cause severe inflammation and eventual scarring from the inflammation. The plaques are a direct result of the pleural scarring.

They are not seen as dangerous. However, they are an indicator of asbestos exposure. They provide a marker that other asbestos diseases may develop in the future.

Diffuse Pleural Thickening

Diffuse pleural thickening are areas of pleural thickening. Simply put, this is the thickening of sections of the lining that surrounds the lung.

The thickening is usually well defined in areas. It is formed on the lining on the chest wall and is tough sinewy in nature. The areas are more widespread across the lung than with pleural plaques and can also involve both layers of the lung lining.

It is caused as the asbestos fibres lodge and then work their way into the outer lining of the lung. It then causes severe inflammation and eventual scarring from the inflammation. The large areas of thickening are a direct result of the pleural scarring.

Due to the widespread scarring, it can cause breathlessness and is more serious than pleural plaques. It is an indicator of past asbestos exposure. It provides a marker that other asbestos diseases may develop in the future.

Asbestosis

Asbestosis is the most widely known asbestos-related disease but is not the biggest killer today. Asbestosis causes the growth of scar like tissue in the lungs themselves and the lining that surrounds them. The asbestos fibres cause mass irritation to the areas affected.

The formed scar tissue is less flexible and cannot expand and contract as easily as a normal lung.

As such, the lung's functions become more difficult. As the lung cannot expand and contract, it becomes more difficult to breathe over time, which places extra stress on the heart. The scarring also compromises blood flow to the lungs, and this in turn causes the heart to enlarge.

All these factors make asbestosis a painful and debilitating disease, which can cause disability and death.

Asbestos-related Lung Cancer

Lung cancer is one of the most common types of cancer. Asbestos-related lung cancers form due to the asbestos being an irritant within the lung. The irritation that occurs causes cancerous changes within the cells of the lung.

The cells change in a short period after exposure. With the continuation of exposure, more cells change and eventually become cancerous.

Workers who have had prolonged exposure to asbestos have a four times greater chance of developing lung cancer.

Asbestos exposure =
4 times greater risk of lung cancer

Asbestos-related lung cancer is like most lung cancers in that it can be debilitating and ultimately lead to death.

Mesothelioma

Mesothelioma is caused by malignant cells developing in the body's protective lining that covers internal organs, which is called the mesothelium. It can affect the lining of the lungs, and the lining of the abdomen.

Mesothelioma can develop from very short exposures to asbestos. The symptoms can include chest pains, shortness of breath, fatigue or a persistent cough.

Mesothelioma can develop into a debilitating disease and ultimately leads to death.

The youngest person to die in the UK of mesothelioma was Sophie Ellis, who died of mesothelioma at the age of 18. She was diagnosed with the disease at the age of only 13.

Where Sophie was exposed to asbestos is unknown and to contract and die from this disease in such a short timescale is very rare.

The asbestos disease epidemic is very real and a major issue in the UK.

CHAPTER BULLET POINTS

- There are five main diseases.
- They are all a result of asbestos exposure.
- People can develop the disease anywhere from 5-50+ years after exposure.
- Disease can develop from short or longer periods of exposure.
- Exposure can lead to debilitating disease and death.

CHAPTER 6

What's the history?

The looking into the past bit

Asbestos has been used for thousands of years – THOUSANDS!

Its use has been found by archaeologists dating back to the Neolithic or New Stone Age around 10,000 years ago. Our ancestors knew the properties of asbestos and mixed it with clay to enhance their pots when firing them to harden. Its uses have been found in pots and shards in Sweden, Finland and Russia.

What does asbestos mean?

The word asbestos means "Inextinguishable" in Greek and was mentioned in ancient writings.

Back in the time of the Greeks and the Romans, both powerful empires talked about asbestos and its resistance to fire and acids, but they also talked about its harmful effects on humans.

To be more precise, it was the effects on their slaves, so we suppose some slaves dying wasn't too much of an issue to them at the time.

What has asbestos been used for?

Asbestos has been used to make rare historical items such as tablecloths and napkins.

It was also used as linings for suits of armour and even as paper and textiles for writings. Many historical manuscripts have been written on asbestos paper.

The ancient Egyptians used asbestos for burial shrouds and candlewicks. Famous explorers, such as Marco Polo, reference being shown materials believed to be made from asbestos cloth.

The UK started using asbestos in the 1700's. Its usage continually increased during the Industrial Revolution in the late 1800's.

This was assisted by the first commercial mine being opened in Canada in 1879.

Although it was being used more and more, it was still relatively expensive to buy, process and manufacture until mining techniques became more advanced in the 1930's.

This was the major turning point for its use, as it became cheap to use almost overnight and it was also better than all the other products being used. These two factors alone are why asbestos became so widespread in use.

The fact it was cheaper and better than other items being used ensured its success. That's the sad thing about asbestos – it does a fantastic job. However, the massive downside is that it's dangerous to all of us.

This didn't stop its use during any time period. The Greeks and Romans had noted that it caused sickness in the workers who spun and weaved it into textiles. These previous acknowledgements were either forgotten or overlooked.

When was asbestos mostly used?

The use of asbestos was at its largest between 1940 and 1970 when it was used heavily in construction, rail and ship building industries.

How much was used in the UK?

The UK imported between 5 and 6 million tonnes of the stuff. We were the **largest** importers of Amosite asbestos and as previously mentioned, we had the **largest** asbestos manufacturing plant in the world.

How many asbestos items are there?

Asbestos has been used in an estimated 5,000+ products and materials. Its use is astounding for how far it has reached and what it has been put into.

Is it banned everywhere?

As of August 2017, there are 195 countries in the world. Of these, there are a mere 55 countries that have an outright ban on the import, supply and use of asbestos!

CHAPTER BULLET POINTS

- Asbestos has been used for thousands of years.
- Asbestos means inextinguishable in ancient Greek.
- Its peak use was between 1940 - 1970.
- It was used because it became cheap and was better than everything else.
- It's been used in over 5,000 products.
- The UK imported the most amosite.
- The UK had the largest manufacturer of asbestos products in the world.
- Only 55 countries out of 195 have banned the total import, supply and use.

CHAPTER 7

Government Regulations

The boring but needed bit

In the UK, there is a hierarchy of Health and Safety Legislation, which has an umbrella type effect that cascades down the chain to the next.

The hierarchy looks like this:

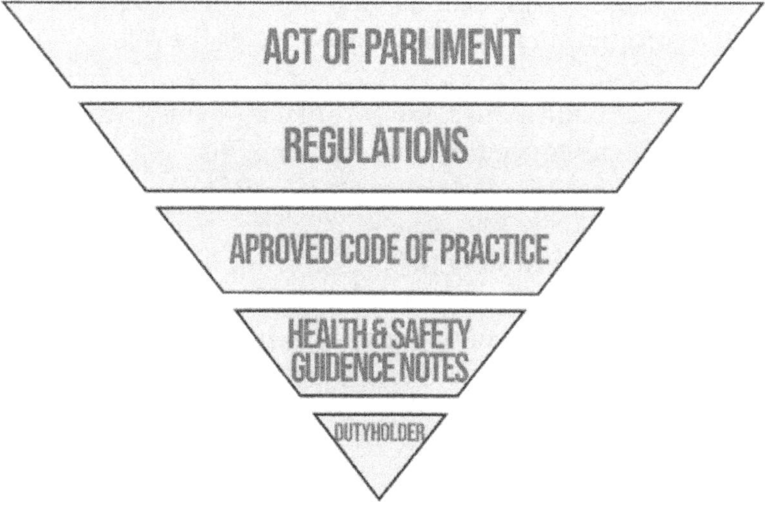

Act of Parliament

An act is the primary piece of legislation. An Act of Parliament must be passed through and agreed upon by Parliament itself.

It also must receive consent from the Queen and only passes as law once it has received both nods of approval. Acts therefore usually take a very long time to bring into fruition.

Regulations

Regulations are known as secondary legislation. Regulations do not require to be passed by Parliament and the Queen.

Acts of Parliament give ministers the power to make Regulations within a particular area under the Act.

Regulations require the same sort of compliance. However, they can be introduced much faster than Acts of Parliament themselves.

Approved Codes of Practice

Approved Codes of Practice, also known as ACoPs, are the recommended or preferred methods or standards that are required to be met.

The ACoPs are written to be in line with the main Regulations and Acts.

By order of following in line with the ACoPs, the Regulations and Acts will also be complied with. They provide insight and guides to what is expected and what is meant in the Regulations and Acts. They provide information such as what is deemed "reasonably practicable".

Reasonably practicable is a term the industry loves to use. If you're familiar with any health and safety guidance documents, we're sure you would have come across it before.

The dictionary meanings for both words are...

Reasonably – to a moderate or acceptable degree.

Practicable – able to be done or put into practice successfully.

In the health and safety world, reasonably practicable usually implies that the "owner" must make a calculation where the scale of risk is measured against what is required in adverting that risk.

<u>RISK</u>
COST, TIME, TROUBLE

In simple terms, think of a scale. On one side is the risk and on the other side is cost, time and trouble to reduce or illuminate the risk. The owner must do as much as possible to tip the scale in favour of illuminating the risk.

Health and Safety Guidance Notes

Health and Safety Guidance Notes are written to interpret what the law states. This interpretation helps the reader to comply with the law.

They also provide technical advice and information and can also prescribe elements of how some items must be completed.

What are the main documents?

The following are the main documents in relation to asbestos. There are other documents that are required to be complied with for different industries, situations or other general Health and Safety requirements that fall outside this list.

UK Prescribed Info	Documentation
Act of Parliament	Health and Safety at Work etc Act 1974
Regulations	Control of Asbestos Regulations 2012
Approved Codes of Practice	L143 Managing and working with asbestos
Health and Safety Guidance Notes	HSG264: Asbestos: The Survey Guide HSG247: Asbestos The Licensed Contractors' Guide HSG248: Asbestos: The Analysts' Guide for Sampling, Analysis and Clearance Procedures HSG 227: A Comprehensive Guide to Managing Asbestos in Premises Asbestos Essentials

All of these documents can be purchased from the Health and Safety Executives book publishing arm. This is the link to the HSE website: www.hse.gov.uk

Alternatively, the documents can also be downloaded for free from the same link.

The PDF versions cover the same material, but are laid out slightly different and also have less photos and illustrations within them. The PDF versions are great.

The content pages hyperlink to the relevant pages and you can search for keywords, which makes these documents easier to use.

As they're electronic, you can keep the full library of documents on your desktop, laptop, tablet or phone.

It's worthwhile noting that although the documents can be downloaded or purchased from the HSE's website, in fact, some of the information held within is now out of date and incorrect!

One of the obvious ones is the references to the CAWR Regulations, which were the old Control of Asbestos at Work Regulations – these are wholly superseded by the CAR 2012 (Control of Asbestos Regulations 2012).

There are other changes within these documents also.

The most ignored regulation!

Probably the most important regulation and reason why you're reading this book is:

Regulation 4: The duty to manage asbestos in non-domestic properties.

Now this regulation was introduced in 2002 and was enforced in 2004. This two-year gap was to give people enough time to get their heads round what they needed to do and give them time to get everything in place. Wow! What an underestimate that was!

Here we are **16 years later** and still a scary amount of people are not compliant, but an even scarier amount have no idea they've even got to do something!

How can this be? The most recent change in regulation was all about data protection.
When we say GDPR, you'll most likely know what we're talking about – even our retired mums know all about it!

To put it bluntly, companies shit themselves about complying with this one, yet when it comes to complying with a regulation that's in place to stop people dying, there's tumbleweeds.

In the next chapter, we'll walk you through our simple seven steps to asbestos compliance.

Let's first look at who the regs apply to and where.

Where does the duty to manage asbestos apply?

The approved code of practice states:

The duty to manage covers all non-domestic premises.

This includes all industrial and commercial buildings such as factories, warehouses, offices and shops.

Public buildings such as hospitals, schools, museums, libraries, leisure centres, churches and other religious buildings.

Also included are road and rail vehicles, vessels, aircraft and offshore installations, as well as structures and installations, such as bridges, street furniture such as street lighting, etc.

The duty does **not** apply to **domestic premises** such as private houses. However, the duty does apply to the "common parts" of multi–occupancy domestic premises such as a block of flats or houses converted into flats.

Examples of common parts may be entrance lobbies, foyers, corridors, lifts, lift shafts, staircases, roof spaces, gardens, yards, outhouses and garages but does not include private domestic areas inside each flat.

Who is responsible for the duty to manage?

The approved code of practice states:

The duty to manage asbestos is placed on the person or organisation that has the overall responsibility for maintenance or repair of a non-domestic premises.

The person who has this responsibility is called the Dutyholder. This can be the owner of the property, the tenant, if they maintain the property, or it could be an agent who manages the property.

The extent of the duty will usually be determined by the degree of responsibility regarding the fabric of the building and the maintenance activities carried out there.

Where these responsibilities are not clear, the duty is placed on whoever has ultimate control of the property.

The dutyholder's legal responsibilities set by the regulations cannot be delegated.

Dutyholders can nominate others to do all or part of the work to assist in complying with regulation. However, they must ensure that the persons they employ are competent to do this work.

In shortened terms these are the basic principles of asbestos management:

Find = identify the location of asbestos

Presume = presume asbestos is present unless it can be proven its not

Protect = protect the asbestos / prevent disturbance

Communicate = communicate all asbestos information to all that need to know

Check = check its condition on a regular basis

Update = update all information so it is always up to date

THE SIX PRINCIPLES OF ASBESTOS MANAGEMENT

- FIND
- PRESUME
- PROTECT
- COMMUNICATE
- CHECK
- UPDATE

CHAPTER BULLET POINTS

- There is a hierarchy of Health and Safety Legislation.
- Act of Parliament must be passed by Parliament and the Queen and can take ages to pass.
- Regulations are passed by Ministers and provide an easier route to legislation than Acts.
- Approved Codes of Practice give an insight and guide to the Act and Regulations.
- Health and Safety Guidance Notes provide interpretation and technical advice.
- Documents can be purchased or downloaded for free.
- Some of the documents have not been updated with information that has changed.
- Regulation 4 – Duty to manage asbestos.
- The duty to manage applies to all non-domestic premises.
- The dutyholder is the person who is responsible for maintenance and repair of a property.

CHAPTER 7 Getting Stuff Done

Download copies of all the documents so you have them to reference:

DOCUMENT AND LINK	✓
HEALTH AND SAFETY AT WORK ETC ACT 1974 *http://www.hse.gov.uk/legislation/hswa.htm*	
CONTROL OF ASBESTOS REGULATIONS 2012 *http://www.hse.gov.uk/asbestos/regulations.htm*	
L143 MANAGING AND WORKING WITH ASBESTOS *http://www.hse.gov.uk/pubns/books/l143.htm*	
L143 MANAGING AND WORKING WITH ASBESTOS Read pages 26 – 38	
HSG264: ASBESTOS: THE SURVEY GUIDE *http://www.hse.gov.uk/pubns/books/hsg264.htm*	
HSG247: ASBESTOS THE LICENSED CONTRACTORS GUIDE *http://www.hse.gov.uk/pubns/books/hsg247.htm*	
HSG248: ASBESTOS: THE ANALYSTS' GUIDE FOR SAMPLING, ANALYSIS AND CLEARANCE PROCEDURES *http://www.hse.gov.uk/pubns/books/hsg248.htm*	
HSG 227: A COMPREHENSIVE GUIDE TO. MANAGING ASBESTOS IN PREMISES *http://www.hse.gov.uk/pubns/books/hsg227.htm*	
ASBESTOS ESSENTIALS *http://www.hse.gov.uk/asbestos/essentials/*	

CHAPTER 8

Where do you start?

Don't worry, we've got your back!

The HSE has bountiful amount of information within their website. However, some of it is not so easy to traverse and understand. As with the rest of this book, our aim is to provide you with the most information in the easiest to understand format.

7 Steps to Asbestos Management Heaven!

The following overview highlights what is required to be fully asbestos compliant with Regulation 4. We have summarised the regulation and what is required.

Step 1. Identify Asbestos
Step 2. Record Findings
Step 3. Assess the Risk
Step 4. Management Plan
Step 5. Make Asbestos Safe
Step 6. Communicating and Sharing
Step 7. Reviewing and Updating

Step 1. Identify Asbestos

Dutyholders are required to identify or presume asbestos materials are present within their property and check their condition.

The easiest way to identify if asbestos materials are present within a property is to have an asbestos survey.

Asbestos surveys will be explained further in the next chapter. However, a management survey is generally used to provide this level of information. As the name suggests, asbestos management surveys provide the asbestos information required to manage asbestos on a day-to-day basis.

A management survey is the easiest route. However, there is the option of presuming asbestos materials. In reality, this is not very practical because we already know that asbestos was used in over 5,000 products – that's a lot of presumptions in a building!

With asbestos management, you have to:

PRESUME IT'S ASBESTOS UNTIL YOU CAN PROVE IT'S NOT!

Without evidence if materials are asbestos or not, you have to presume everything is. In reality, this is just not practical to operate on a day-to-day basis within your property and/or business.

Any material known or presumed to contain asbestos must be kept in a good state of repair. Therefore, the condition of the asbestos materials must be assessed. This assessment is called a material risk assessment.

This book advocates that the dutyholder can complete a lot of things themselves. However, some things we believe should be left to the experts.

It makes no sense for a layperson to take the risk of identifying asbestos-containing materials on their own. In UKAS, accredited companies' surveyors are only let loose once they are deemed competent to do so – see Chapter 9 for more info on competence and UKAS accredited surveyors.

It is, however, the dutyholder's responsibility to ensure that the survey completed is to the correct standard – again, further info in Chapter 8 is provided.

Step 2. Record Findings

Dutyholders are required to ensure that a written record of the asbestos is made and that the record is **kept up to date**.

A written record, usually referred to as an asbestos register, and site plan detailing asbestos locations, presumed locations and areas not accessed should be completed.

Again, the easiest way to complete this is with a management survey! Or you can get your pen and paper out and get writing, a lot! For your own assessment to be worth its weight, it will need to have been completed in line with *HSG264: Asbestos The Surveyors Guide.* As previously mentioned, guidance complies with ACoPs, Regulations and Acts, which we want to stay on the right side of.

Once the survey or written records (register and drawing plans) have been completed, they MUST be kept up to date. All too often dutyholders have surveys completed but fail to do anything beyond this point.

The register and plans must be live documents all up to date and reflect the current conditions. If the condition of the asbestos changes (material risk changes), if asbestos materials are removed and even if areas of the building change, these documents must be updated.

Step 3. Assess the Risk

Dutyholders are required to assess the risk of anyone being exposed to these asbestos materials.

Managing asbestos means preventing people from breathing in asbestos fibres. Assessing the likelihood of exposure to asbestos will help you to comply with your legal duties.

Priority Risk Assessments (PRAs) can help you determine the likely risk of people being exposed to asbestos from the materials present within your building. Or, in other words, help you identify the risk of the asbestos being disturbed by someone in your building and them being exposed to it.

These assessments also help you to set a priority as to what needs to be actioned first. The overall risk is determined from the risk of the material and the risk to the occupants.

This one should be a joint approach at least. You can save money and time by having the asbestos surveyor complete these for you. The cost increase to complete PRAs is usually negligible. However, the most important aspect of having these completed by the surveyor is to then go through them and check they are correct!

The surveyor can only use their best guess when completing these. Therefore, it is imperative that you check the data. After all, you know your building and you'll have a better knowledge of its occupants and activities within it.

If you want to save money or if you want to gauge a real understanding about PRAs, you can complete them either by following the steps in HSG264. Or you can use the PRA tool, which can be found here:

https://tinyurl.com/yceu8vdv

This form allows you to use the information from the survey and to then generate your own PRAs. Or you can use this to check the PRAs that have been completed on your behalf by the surveying company.

Step 4. Asbestos Management Plan

Dutyholders are required to ensure that a written plan to manage the asbestos risk is prepared and that the plan is put into effect.

The asbestos management plan (AMP) should set out how the identified asbestos risks should be managed. The most important thing here is whatever you plan to do you must put into action.

Depending upon your site, this is going to be really easy or really difficult to put together.

Further information on AMPs has been written in its own chapter later in this book (Chapter 12).

Step 5. Make Asbestos Safe

Dutyholders are required to ensure that any material known or presumed to contain asbestos is managed accordingly. Factors, such as the location, condition and frequency of access, will determine the action required e.g., repair, physical protection or removal.

Asbestos works may need to be completed following appropriate assessments. An appropriate contractor who is trained, insured and/or licensed to work with asbestos will be required.

Certain types of works will also require accredited independent asbestos air testing. More information on asbestos works is discussed in Chapter 11.

The main purpose for asbestos work isn't to remove asbestos unless it's necessary – it should be to ensure that it's safe and manageable.

Step 6. Communicating and Sharing

Dutyholders are required to ensure that information regarding the asbestos is provided to anyone who is liable to disturb it or potentially at risk.

Asbestos information must be provided by the dutyholder to anyone likely to come into contact with asbestos in their buildings.

This can be achieved in a number of ways, e.g. hard copies of surveys, electronic copies of surveys and online asbestos survey databases.

Again, depending upon the size and complexity of the estate, one or more ways may be required to ensure the information is shared accordingly.

Databases should no longer be expensive to buy or to utilise. We provide a FREE online database for all our clients – it's included in the price for whatever we complete.

There are database companies still charging exorbitant fees for setup and use per gigabyte storage. In a predominantly online world that we now live in, this simply shouldn't be charged for.

The only times that fees should be incurred are when the system is needed to do something out of the ordinary and the developer's time is needed.

For a standard online database, you should be paying **ZERO, £0.00, NOTHING**! We have clients with thousands upon thousands of sites held and their cost is **ZILCH**.

Step 7. Reviews and Updates

As a minimum, the asbestos management plan, including records and drawings, should be reviewed and updated every 12 months.

Annual asbestos reinspections and annual management plan audits should be undertaken.

Again, this is something you may be able to do if you are competent. However, it would be our recommendation to utilise a surveying company for the same reasons as getting a survey undertaken.

It eliminates your risk and also saves time because all documents associated with the reinspection need to be updated, along with the Asbestos Register, AMP, the PRAs and also the online database.

CHAPTER BULLET POINTS

There are seven steps to asbestos management:

Step 1. Identify Asbestos.

Step 2. Record Findings.

Step 3. Assess the Risk.

Step 4. Management Plan.

Step 5. Make Asbestos Safe.

Step 6. Communicating and Sharing.

Step 7. Reviewing and Updating.

CHAPTER 8 Getting Stuff Done

Use this list as a basic tick list. Start collating what information you have and you will soon be fully managing your asbestos.

DOCUMENT	✓
IDENTIFY ASBESTOS = (ASBESTOS SURVEY REPORT)	
RECORD FINDINGS = (ASBESTOS SURVEY REPORT)	
RISK ASSESSMENTS = (ASBESTOS SURVEY REPORT)	
MANAGEMENT PLAN = CREATE OR CONSULTANT TO ASSIST	
ASBESTOS WORKS = REVIEW REPORT AND SPEC ANY WORKS	
COMMUNICATING AND SHARING = PASS ON INFORMATION	
REVIEW AND UPDATE = AMP AND REINSPECTION 12 MONTHS	

CHAPTER 9

Asbestos Surveys

What survey do you need?

There are different types of asbestos surveys, each specific to the task in hand. Understanding the difference between them is key.

Asbestos surveys were previously known as Type 1, Type 2, Type 3 surveys. This was confusing for clients as the terminologies were non-descriptive.

In 2010, with the introduction of *HSG 264 Asbestos: The Survey Guide*, the survey types were renamed.

Management Survey

Refurbishment Survey

Demolition Survey

The guidance describes Refurbishment and Demolition surveys under the same heading, which led to some confusion within the industry. This has led to companies calling intrusive surveys refurbishment and demolition surveys or R&D surveys.

However, these are two different surveys and should be referred to accordingly.

Management Surveys

A management survey is the entry-level survey. Its purpose is to locate and describe asbestos within a building.

The survey should record the extent and condition of asbestos materials. It should access all areas in the building that could be damaged or disturbed during day-to-day occupancy. This should cover areas where you would expect a maintenance person to access.

Visual inspections of ceilings, walls, floors, accessible ducts, service risers, lofts, etc.
Although these surveys are non-destructive, minor decorative damage will occur from sampling of any suspect materials.

Management Survey Summary

- Used to provide information for managing asbestos in a premises.
- Find asbestos during normal occupancy of a building.
- Access everywhere a maintenance person would generally go.
- Sampling survey.
- Not destructive.

Refurbishment Surveys

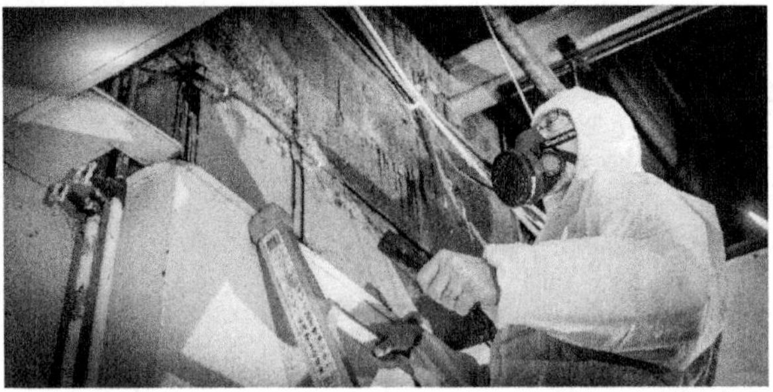

A refurbishment survey, as the name suggests, is required prior to any intrusive refurbishment works.

They are used to locate and describe all asbestos within a building or part of a building.

By nature, these types of survey are intrusive and, to a degree, destructive. For example, it is important to know what the insulation materials are in a wall cavity.

These surveys are also undertaken in situations where destructive maintenance activities are required such as during boiler and heating upgrade works.

Refurbishment surveys are designed to access hidden parts of the building in line with the overall scope of works for the refurbishment.

The key to these surveys is having a fully detailed and confirmed scope of works.

Existing and proposed plans will assist the surveyors to ensure all areas are accessed.

Equally important, this will prevent any unnecessary damage to areas not included in the refurbishment.

Refurbishment Survey Summary

- Used to identify asbestos that may be hidden.
- Before any refurbishment works or before intrusive maintenance and repair works e.g., plant dismantling.
- Disturbance of the fabric of the building.
- Fully intrusive and destructive in line with specification.

Demolition Surveys

A demolition survey, as the name suggests, is required to be undertaken prior to demolition of a building.

These types of survey are fully intrusive and extremely destructive. They are used to locate and describe all asbestos within a building.

In line with the guidance, demolition is only utilised as a descriptive when a building is to be demolished and removed in its entirety.

Therefore, when an asbestos demolition survey is requested, the scope of works is self-explanatory.

In addition to areas inspected within a management survey, areas hidden within the structure of the building will be accessed. For example, beneath carpets & floor coverings, within walls & ceilings, behind claddings & partitions, within structural supports and within lofts & floor voids.

Demolition Survey Summary

- Used to identify ALL asbestos that may be hidden.
- Before complete demolition of a building.
- Totally intrusive and destructive.
- Designed to access all areas of the building.
- Usually cannot be occupied after survey.

Asbestos Building Life Cycle

This graphic shows the life cycle of a building in relation to asbestos.

Management Surveys
Usually properties start at the management survey stage.

Minor Refurbishment Surveys
Which then move on to minor refurbishments taking place over time.

Major Refurbishment Surveys
Then maybe a huge revamp of the property happens where an extensive asbestos refurbishment survey is undertaken.

Demolition Survey
The building then comes to the end of its life and a fully extensive demolition survey is undertaken. This also may require the use of surveyors assisting the demolition contractor.

Complete Knowledge
Only when the building has been completely demolished and everything removed, including footings and all services disconnected, etc., can we then look back and review the overall asbestos picture of the site.

How do you choose a surveyor?

Competence for Surveys

Competence is the key for achieving an appropriate asbestos survey.

This is the most important thing in the chain of events for asbestos management – it cannot be underestimated. The asbestos actually needs to be found in order for it to be managed!

The HSE "strongly recommend" the use of accredited or certified surveyors. In reality, that gives you two options of UKAS accredited or not. There were schemes set up to incorporate one-man band surveyors. However, the uptake was poor and therefore each version of the schemes were scrapped.

If we were dutyholder's looking to sort out our asbestos and the HSE strongly recommended something, we wouldn't do anything else – why would you!? It's the HSE and they've said it for a reason.

Accredited by UKAS proves that the company has achieved a benchmarked level, so you can take reassurance that they have at the least met a basic standard. That said, however, there should be a massive **BUYER BEWARE** sign in the fact that not all organisations and all individuals within UKAS accredited companies are at the same level.

Just because a business has UKAS accreditation, it does not mean that you can negate your duties in ensuring they can do the job.

How much will an asbestos survey cost?

Asbestos surveys can be expensive.

Reputable companies ensure surveys are undertaken by experienced and competent surveyors, that enough samples are collected and analysed, that they have the correct level of insurances (which are extremely expensive) and that they maintain all the accreditations and relevant professional memberships required.

Therefore, going for the cheapest is not always a wise move. You should always do your homework and check the company out before letting them loose within your properties.

The asbestos industry is the same as any industry in that you get the good, the bad and the downright rubbish all trying to make a living.

The UKAS stamp of approval does provide some level of confidence. However, there are still more things that you can do to ensure you've tried your best to get the right job completed the first time.

Competence is deemed as a combination of training, skills, experience and knowledge. This can easily be quantified and broken down into its various elements to be measured against.

In UKAS organisations, the minimum requirement to become a surveyor is six months' experience plus the relevant qualification from RSPH or the BOHS. In addition to this, they are required to prove their competence by successfully passing multiple internal audits.

Competence is required to be proven over each building category (Domestic, Commercial or Industrial) and for each survey type (Management, Refurbishment & Demolition).

In theory, non-accredited surveyors could pass the course and crack on with very little experience and knowledge - but in the eyes of the client they hold the same training certificate, so they must be ok, right?

We would suggest checking the competence of whomever you employ for your surveys, whether a UKAS organisation or non-accredited surveyor. In fact, the UKAS companies should be checked, but as well as the business, you should be checking the actual surveyor who will be allocated to your works.

If the site is a simple office, this may not be as important. However, if your site is a massive factory or hospital, then the surveyor working within these should have a proven record in surveying this type of property.

The organisation may have the skills and expertise. However, it is best to check that the expertise you require will be deployed to carry out your actual work.

To identify these things, there are multiple things you can do to gauge the level and instil confidence in the company or individual undertaking your surveys.

The following are the types of items that could be checked:

Assemble your asbestos POWER TEAM!

Credit Check
Credit check the business – are they buoyant with good cash flow?

Training
Provide an explanation re: the surveyor's time served in training prior to undertaking asbestos surveys.

Qualifications
What asbestos surveying qualifications does the surveyor hold?

Experience
Provide details of time carrying out asbestos surveys in the field.

Proven Experience
What's the auditing process for surveyors and how many audits are completed for Domestic, Commercial, Industrial survey types?

References
Ask for at least two references of people whom the company has carried out similar surveying work and would be willing to have a call with them.

Risk Assessments
What are their anticipated risk assessments for the surveying tasks at the site?

Independence, impartiality and integrity
Provide copies of policies to confirm what is in place and how these are checked.

Quality Management System
Provide details of their quality management system and detail how these are checked.

Surveying Methodology
Confirm what surveying methodology they plan to work to.

CPD
Detail how the surveyors and staff undertake continual professional development.

Audits
Describe the audit procedure that is in place for completed asbestos surveys.

Survey Reinspections
Describe the reinspection procedure of surveys completed.

Example Report
Provide an example of a completed report for the same style of survey that is to be carried out (Management, Refurbishment, Demolition).
The report is the end product – it's what you'll be left with and will need to use. Make sure it's in a format you're happy with and can use.

Don't be afraid to ask for the report to be produced in a format that works for you!

Once you have answers to all of the questions from the companies you plan to use, you can then sit and review them collectively marking off things you like, things you don't and any concerns you have.

Do whatever you feel necessary to feel comfortable with the organisations. Even go as far as getting on the phone to them and having a chat, not just with the smooth-talking sales team or the Op's manager. Ask to speak to the actual surveyor they plan to use on your work.

Check out what they have to say about the company and see if what they are saying resonates with the documentation you have been sent.

If feasible, request and then pay a visit to their offices and chat to the staff. Likewise, do the same with the referees they have suggested, pick up the phone and have a ten-minute chat with them. You will be certain to glean information, which will no doubt convince you one way or the other.

Price has not been mentioned yet, which is always a factor. This should not come into it until you have identified the surveying companies you would do business with.

We've all heard someone say either in a movie or in the real world "it's nothing personal, it's just business", which sounds great as a one-liner. However, business is personal!

This has to be the main factor when working with someone – you have to get along, have the confidence in them and also know that you can sort out problems if something goes awry.

Once you have your shortlist of contractors you want to work with, you can then look at price.

Far too many organisations say they want an all singing and all dancing organisation. All procurement procedures are "followed" right up until the price point comes into play and then it's almost as if everything else is dropped and just the cost is reviewed.

This is another **BUYER BEWARE** scenario in that you get what you pay for. It's like buying anything – you get different standards and different levels of service. You need to determine what you want before going out to market.

The asbestos industry is like any other in that you get bottom of the barrel prices right up to champagne prices, but with each end of the scale, you will receive totally different experiences.

What do you really want? Do you like contractual fighting over every little element because the business' margins are so tight that every little thing is an "extra"?

Or do you like being taken to the rugby every week on the client account knowing that ultimately you are paying for it?

Or maybe a middle of the road approach whereby you don't mind getting involved with contractual wranglings a little and knowing your call would be answered and issue sorted?

Once you've decided on your desired outcome, you can then bring cost in because ultimately to get more you will pay more, however the desired outcome should be the overriding factor.

CHAPTER BULLET POINTS

- Surveyor competence is key.
- HSE strongly recommend UKAS accredited surveyors.
- Various steps can be followed to check competence.
- Cost will vary depending on your desired outcome.

CHAPTER 9 Getting Stuff Done

Surveyor Competency Checklist

All elements covered in this chapter have been turned into a form, which can be downloaded and edited with your logo and data added.

Send this to the surveying company to complete and ask them to send you copies of everything required.

Visit the following webpage to download a copy:

www.asbestosthedarkarts.com/asbestos-surveyor-competence-check

Insert Your Logo Here

Asbestos Surveyor Competence Check

Any section relating to specific qualifications and training must be completed about the actual surveyor who will be undertaking the proposed survey. To be sent to the surveying company to complete:

Contractor Name and Address			
Training – provide an explanation re the surveyor's time served in training prior to undertaking asbestos surveys.			
Qualifications – what asbestos surveying qualifications does the surveyor hold.			
CCP Asbestos	BOHS P402	RSPH Surveying	Other Relevant Quals
Experience – provide details of time carrying out asbestos surveys in the field			
Proven Experience – describe your auditing process for surveyors and how many audits are completed for Domestic, Commercial, Industrial survey types			
References – Provide contact details for at least 2 people whom you have carried out similar surveying work			
Name		Name	
Number		Number	
Email		Email	
Previous Job details		Previous Job details	
Risk Assessments – What will be your anticipated risk assessments for the surveying tasks at the site?			
Independence, impartiality and integrity - Provide copies of your policies to confirm what is in place and how these are checked.			
Quality Management System – Provide details of your quality management system and detail how these are checked.			
Surveying Methodology – confirm what surveying methodology you prescribe to, detail techniques and any reference documentation used.			

CHAPTER 9 Getting Stuff Done

Asbestos Survey Report Checklist

All elements covered in this chapter have been turned into a form, which can be downloaded and edited with your logo and data added.

Use this form to check the asbestos survey report contains everything it should.

Visit the following webpage to download a copy:

www.asbestosthedarkarts.com/Asbestos-Survey-Report-Check

Insert Your Logo Here

Asbestos Survey Report Check

The following can be completed to check the main elements that are most important and should be found within an asbestos survey report. Make notes on any section that you need to question the surveying company with to be satisfied that the report is fit for purpose:

Site Name and Address / Reference Number
Site name and address details / your reference number for the project etc. This form can be placed within your files to prove you have checked the report contents.

Checklist	☒	☑
Does the report determine what type of survey was carried out and is this correct?	☐	☐
Comments:		
Does the report determine the site surveyed and is this correct?	☐	☐
Comments:		
Does the report contain an executive summary?	☐	☐
Comments:		
Does the report contain an introduction and scope of the survey?	☐	☐
Comments:		

CHAPTER 10

What is an asbestos risk assessment?

How do you assess the risk?

When most people hear the word "Risk Assessment" they make a big sigh and they think ballache. Does that sound familiar?

We want to change that feeling for you. Especially when it comes to Priority Risk Assessments.

These bad boys are not that complicated and can save you some significant amounts of cash if completed correctly. And guess what? We're going to show you how in this chapter.

What are Material and Priority Risk Assessments?

First, the basics. There are two types of assessments when evaluating the overall risk from asbestos – Material Risk Assessments and Priority Risk Assessments.

Materials Risk Assessments

A material risk assessment assesses the condition of the material and the likelihood of it releasing asbestos fibres should it be disturbed. In other words, how easy will that material release asbestos fibres if it was to be damaged.

Material risk assessments should be provided as part of any survey you have completed, although survey guidance has always stated that material risk assessments are not required as part of refurbishment or demolition surveys, unless the period between the survey and the event is significant, e.g., more than three months.

In a combined 31 years of industry experience, we have only seen probably two surveys where these assessments haven't been completed.

Material risk assessments are determined by using a simple algorithm set out in HSE guidance document *HSG264 Asbestos: The Survey Guide.*

The algorithm looks at four parameters:

Product Type
(Type of product the material is)

Damage Extent or Deterioration
(How damaged the material is)

Surface Treatment
(How the material is sealed)

Asbestos Type
(Type of asbestos fibre present in the material. Scored worst case.)

Each parameter is scored between 1 and 3.

Two parameters can be scored 0.

The scores are added up to provide the score, which falls into one of four categories:

10 or more have a high potential to release asbestos fibre.

7-9 have a medium potential to release asbestos fibre.

5-6 have a low potential to release asbestos fibre.
4 or less have a very low potential to release asbestos fibre.

Stating the bloody obvious... but non-asbestos materials have no potential to release asbestos fibre.

Material Risk Assessment Table

Product Type

Score	Examples
1	Asbestos reinforced composites (plastics, resins, mastics, roofing, felts, vinyl floor tiles, semi rigid paints or decorative finishes, asbestos cement, etc.)
2	Asbestos insulating board, mill boards, other low density insulation boards, asbestos textiles, gaskets, ropes and woven textiles, asbestos paper and felt.
3	Thermal insulation (e.g., pipe and boiler lagging), sprayed asbestos, loose asbestos, asbestos mattresses and packing.

Damage Extent

Score	Examples
0	Good condition: no visible damage.
1	Low damage: a few scratches or surface marks; broken edges on boards, tiles, etc.
2	Medium damage: significant breakage of materials or several small areas where material has been damaged revealing loose fibres.
3	High damage or delamination of materials, sprays and thermal insulation. Visible asbestos debris.

Surface Treatment

Score	Examples
0	Composite materials containing asbestos: reinforced plastics, resins, vinyl tiles.
1	Enclosed sprays and lagging, AIB (with exposed face painted or encapsulated), asbestos cement sheets, etc.
2	Unsealed AIB or encapsulated lagging and sprays.
3	Unsealed lagging and sprays.

Asbestos Type

Score	Examples
1	Chrysotile
2	Amphibole asbestos excluding Crocidolite
3	Crocidolite

Example Material Assessment 1:

Asbestos floor tiles, good condition in an average sized occupied office.

Product Type	**1** = Vinyl floor tiles
Damage Extent	**0** = Good condition
Surface Treatment	**0** = Composite materials/vinyl tiles
Asbestos Type	**1** = Chrysotile
Material Assessment Score	**2** = 4 or less have a very low potential to release asbestos fibre.
Based on a score of 2, the asbestos floor tiles could be managed in their current state and condition without needing any works to make safe.	

Example Material Assessment 2:

Asbestos pipe insulation, badly damaged in an average sized disused boiler room:

Product Type	**3** = Thermal insulation
Damage Extent	**3** = High damage/thermal insulation. Visible asbestos debris.
Surface Treatment	**3** = Unsealed lagging
Asbestos Type	**2** = Amphibole asbestos excluding Crocidolite
Material Assessment Score	**11** = 10 or more have a high potential to release asbestos fibre.
Based on a score of 11, the asbestos pipe insulation would need to be repaired or removed, and the asbestos debris would require removing. The area should also be locked and kept out of bounds to all personnel until it's made safe.	

Priority Risk Assessments

A priority risk assessment assesses the likelihood of an asbestos material being disturbed. In other words, what's the risk of someone being exposed to asbestos fibre from that material?

The purpose of this assessment is to help prioritise actions that may be required to manage the asbestos.

The priority assessment should be completed by someone who has good knowledge of the building, its use and occupancy.

Now these assessments can be completed by an asbestos surveyor who can have a good guess, but it will never be 100% accurate. The "dutyholder" i.e., the person responsible, should ensure these assessments are as accurate as possible.

Priority risk assessments are determined by using a simple algorithm set out in HSE guidance document *HSG227 A comprehensive guide to Managing Asbestos in premises.*

The priority risk assessment takes into account the following factors:

Occupant Activity
(What type of activities are completed within the area?)

Likelihood of Disturbance
(How easily will the material be damaged based on its location, accessibility and size?)

Human Exposure Potential
(The scale of how many people will potentially be exposed to the material, how often and for how long.)

Maintenance Activity
(What types of maintenance activities are likely to happen within the area of the material and how frequent they are? Meaning, how likely is the material to be damaged by routine maintenance works?)

How do you Complete a Priority Risk Assessment?

The following table describes the basic considerations to be taken into account when evaluating the overall priority risk.

Priority Risk Assessment Table

Occupant Activity

Assessment Factor:	Score:	Examples of Score Variables:
Main Activity: Main type of activity in area	0	Rare disturbance activity (e.g., little used store room)
	1	Low disturbance activities (e.g., office type activity)
	2	Periodic disturbance (e.g., industrial or vehicular activity which may contact ACMs)
	3	High levels of disturbance (e.g., fire door with asbestos insulating board sheet in constant use)
Secondary Activity:	As Above	As Above

Likelihood of Disturbance

Assessment Factor:	Score:	Examples of Score Variables:
Location:	0	Outdoors
	1	Large rooms or well ventilated areas
	2	Rooms up to 100m^2
	3	Confined spaces
Accessibility:	0	Usually inaccessible or unlikely to be disturbed
	1	Occasionally likely to be disturbed
	2	Easily disturbed
	3	Routinely disturbed
Extent/Amount	0	Small amounts or items (e.g., strings, gaskets)
	1	<10 m^2 or <10 Lm
	2	>10 m^2 to <50m^2 or >10 Lm to <50 Lm
	3	>50 m^2 or >50 Lm

Priority Risk Assessment Table Continued

Human Exposure Potential

Assessment Factor:	Score:	Examples of Score Variables:
Number of Occupants:	0	None
	1	1 to 3
	2	4 to 10
	3	>10
Frequency of Area Usage:	0	Infrequent
	1	Monthly
	2	Weekly
	3	Daily
Average Time Area in Use Per Day:	0	< 1 Hour
	1	> 1 Hour to < 3 Hours
	2	> 3 Hour to < 6 Hours
	3	> 6 Hours

Maintenance Activity

Assessment Factor:	Score:	Examples of Score Variables:
Type of Maintenance Activity:	0	Minor disturbance (e.g., access)
	1	Low disturbance (e.g., changing light bulbs)
	2	Medium disturbance (e.g., lift asbestos tiles)
	3	High levels of disturbance (e.g., removal of ACM)
Frequency of Maintenance Activity:	0	ACM unlikely to be disturbed for maintenance
	1	<1 per year
	2	>1 per year
	3	>1 per month

Try to be consistent when scoring. However, it's important to remember that this is a guide to help you decide what to do with your asbestos.

The scores are added up to provide the total score, which should then be used to prioritise planning and works of the items dealing with the highest numbers first and working down as they show the greatest risk to occupants.

X3 sections have sub headings and sub scores. The score for these subs are averaged and rounded up.

Example Priority Assessment 1
Low risk material in a high-risk area

Asbestos floor tiles, good condition in an average sized occupied office.

Occupant Activity	**Main Activity:** Main type of activity in area	**1** = Low disturbance activities (e.g., office type activity)	**Overall Score:** **1**
Likelihood of Disturbance	**Location:**	**2** = Rooms up to 100m^2	**Average** **= 2**
	Accessibility:	**0** = Usually inaccessible or unlikely to be disturbed	
	Extent/Amount	**3** = >50 m^2	
Human Exposure Potential	**Number of Occupants:**	**3** = >10	**Average** **= 3**
	Frequency of Area Usage:	**3** = Daily	
	Average Time Area in Use Per Day:	**3** = > 6 Hours	
Maintenance Activity	**Type of Maintenance Activity:**	**0** = Minor disturbance (e.g., access)	**Average** **= 0**
	Frequency of Maintenance Activity:	**0** = ACM unlikely to be disturbed for maintenance	
		Total Priority Score	6
		Material assessment score from survey	2
		Total material and priority scores	**8**

Based on the total score of 8, the floor tiles fall lower than the pipe insulation in priority listing. However, these can still be managed in their current state and condition without needing any works to make safe. They would fall into an annual reinspection program.

Example Priority Assessment 2
High risk material in a low risk area

Asbestos pipe insulation, badly damaged in an average sized disused boiler room:

Occupant Activity	**Main Activity:** Main type of activity in area	**2** = Periodic disturbance (e.g., industrial or vehicular activity, which may contact ACMs)	**Overall Score:** **0**
Likelihood of Disturbance	**Location:**	**2** = Rooms up to $100m^2$	
	Accessibility:	**2** = Easily disturbed	
	Extent/Amount	**2** = >10 Lm to <50 Lm	**Average** **= 2**
Human Exposure Potential	**Number of Occupants:**	**0** = None	
	Frequency of Area Usage:	**0** = Infrequent	
	Average Time Area in Use Per Day:	**0** = < 1 Hour	**Average** **= 0**
Maintenance Activity	**Type of Maintenance Activity:**	**0** = Minor disturbance (e.g., access)	
	Frequency of Maintenance Activity:	**0** = ACM unlikely to be disturbed for maintenance	**Average** **= 0**
		Total Priority Score	2
		Material assessment score from survey	11
		Total material and priority scores	**13**

Based on the total score of 15, the pipe insulation sits higher than the floor tiles in priority listing.

However, the recommendation could possibly be changed, as it's an unused boiler room. This could be locked and sealed and could fall into an annual reinspection program instead of having repair/removal works done on something that is not used.

CHAPTER 10 Getting Stuff Done

Priority Risk Assessment Tool

If you are inclined to carry out your own PRAs or want to check the ones you have, you can check your Priority Risk Assessment in three easy steps.

The following link is to a priority risk assessment form that is made up of three sections.

Complete all sections, hit print PDF and get your completed PRA.

https://tinyurl.com/yceu8vdv

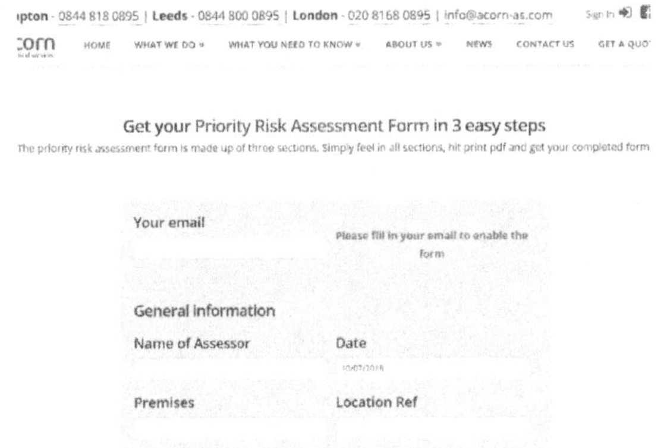

CHAPTER 11

Asbestos Works

How do you get the correct work completed?

Specification is the bible! That's the #1 thing to get right when it comes to asbestos works. What is your desired outcome from the works?

Whatever you do, do not let the asbestos contractor take the lead and just quote you for the "bits" identified in the report.

They need to price for exactly what your requirements are. Otherwise, they'll just price for what they think is nearest to what you want, is relatively easy to do and that you'll get your wallet out for!

Over the years, there have been lots of phrases coined to sound exciting and to try and describe a level of work.

However, in reality they mean different things to different people depending upon who trained them and the company they work for.
Probably one of the most banded about terms used is the dreaded:

"Environmental Clean"

What does environmental clean mean?

To some people, that means vacuum the localised area where debris is located.

To others, it means setting the whole area up as an asbestos enclosure, cleaning every surface, item, as well as removing and disposing of all non-cleanable items and insulation, etc.

That is the problem with using these terms, as they mean different things to different people.

As you can imagine, these two interpretations of the same statement are at complete opposite ends of the spectrum in terms of end result and cost!

Another term used and not confirmed is:

"Encapsulate"

What does encapsulate mean?

To some, that means place boarding over or wrapping asbestos to protect it. To others, it means painting.

The painting one is interesting depending upon who you speak to. Also, some contractors will happily paint with trade emulsion whereas others will use vapour barrier paints, which dry with a slightly rubberised finish to afford slight abrasions.

How many coats of paint will they give it?
Again, it depends on the contractor and what they usually do – that is unless there is a specification for the works. The specification or scope of works should be item specific. This is the only way of guaranteeing you will get what you want. Otherwise, you are giving it over to luck and the judgement of the contractor.

They will have different views as to what's required. Therefore, you need to set the parameters.

This isn't that complicated. It just needs breaking down into what the final desired outcome looks like.

<u>Example: Boiler room with insulation residue to the walls</u>

Are you bothered about what the boiler room looks like on completion? A wall scrape and wire brush under fully controlled conditions may work for you.

Do you need it as "asbestos free" as possible? Garnet or ice blasting may work.

Do you just need to make it safe? If so, encapsulation and labelling may be the right route to go down.

There are always a number of factors that determine why the work is needed, which determines what work is required.

There's no point scraping the walls in a boiler room to receive a certificate that the analyst has caveated with "all lumps removed, asbestos may be present beneath brick paint/within mortar joints".

Yes, the risk of the loose asbestos has gone. However, how will your new boiler replacement works proceed if the plumbers can't fix it to the walls?

The specification should detail in layman's terms what the requirements are. If it's to allow future trades to fix into the walls, then write this down.

If it's to make the boiler room look good as well as making it safe, then write it down. The more complicated, the longer and more complex specifications are required. However, a lot of asbestos remedials can be quoted for accordingly with a basic brief or simple specification.

Example: Encapsulation Simple Brief

The contractor is to neatly encapsulate the ceiling with two coats of white vapour barrier paint.

All of the boiler room walls are to be encapsulated neatly with two coats of grey vapour barrier paint.

The asbestos pipes are to be repaired with new insulation and wrapped with new calico and neatly painted with red high temperature paint.
The walls and pipes are to be labelled with tri-band asbestos warning labels every 1m.

The boiler room floor and plinths are to be painted with grey floor paint.

It's not overly complicated, but it details how you wish the boiler room to be left on completion of the job.

If the contractor has any issue with your spec, they will undoubtedly question you and provide alternative options if what you have asked for isn't wholly achievable.

When requesting encapsulation, you need to highlight the fact that you want the job completed neatly. Contractors will state they are not painters and decorators and that vapour barrier paint is difficult to use.

Both of these are totally true. However, they can take their time and get it looking neat rather than a dog's dinner – it can be achieved.

Again, a large factor in getting the right job completed for the right price is all about getting the right contractor on board.

In a similar fashion to ensuring you have the right asbestos surveyor on board, you can make similar checks to the asbestos contractor prior to proceeding to pricing for works.

We would say at this point, there are some poor licensed asbestos contractors out there.

However, there are good ones and some really good ones. We work with, in our view, some of the best asbestos contractors in the industry.

So how do you identify a good asbestos contractor from a poor one? There are multiple things you can do to gauge the level and instil confidence in the company undertaking the asbestos remedial or removal works.

The following are the types of items that could be checked:

Assemble your asbestos POWER TEAM!

Credit Check

Credit check the business. Are they buoyant with a good cash flow?

HSE Licence
Visit the HSE website and check the licence. Also, check there are no additional conditions on the licence.

ISO Accreditations
Request certificates.

Insurance Cover
Check minimum policies required for the project. Ensure cover is to a decent amount vs. risk.

ARCA/ACAD Member
Confirm member details and confirm the associations' joining criteria.

CHAS/Constructionline/Achilles/Exor
Confirm member details and confirm the joining criteria.

CRB Checks
Are staff suitable for the works? Are there any persons of risk on site/coming to the site?

Plan of Work and Risk Assessments
Request a POW and RA for the project. Does this cover perceived risks on site? Have they thought about equipment locations and DCU transit routes? Can a direct connection be used?

References
Request references for similar works.

Training
Provide an explanation re: the supervisor's time served in training prior to undertaking asbestos supervision of asbestos projects.

Qualifications
What asbestos qualifications does the contracts manager and supervisor hold?

Experience Contracts Manager
Provide details of time carrying out asbestos removal contract management.

Experience Supervisor
Provide details of time carrying out asbestos removal supervision. Must be re: the supervisor who will be running the project.

Proven Experience
Describe your auditing process for removal projects.

References
Ask for at least two references of people whom the company has carried out similar work for and would be willing to have a call with them.

Risk Assessments
What will be your anticipated risk assessments for the tasks at the site?

Independence, Impartiality and Integrity
Provide copies of their policies to confirm what is in place and how these are checked.

Quality Management System
Provide details of their quality management system and detail how these are checked.

CPD
Detail how the contract managers and site staff undertake continual professional development.

There is a little replication in the following paragraphs to that of checking surveying companies out. However, it's because the process is predominantly the same.

Once you have answers to all of the questions from the companies you plan to use, you can then sit and review them collectively marking off things you like, things you don't and any concerns you have.

Do whatever you feel necessary to feel comfortable with the organisations. Even go as far as getting on the phone to them and having a chat, not just with the smooth-talking sales team or the Op's manager. Ask to speak to the actual supervisor and contracts manager they plan to use on your work.

Check out what they have to say about the company and see if what they are saying resonates with the documentation you have been sent.

If feasible, request and then pay a visit to their offices and chat to the staff. Likewise, do the same with the referees they have suggested, pick up the phone and have a ten-minute chat with them. You will be certain to glean information, which will no doubt either convince you one way or the other.

Price has not been mentioned yet, which is always a factor. This should not come into it until you have identified the companies you would do business with. We've all heard someone say either in a movie or in the real world "it's nothing personal, it's just business", which sounds great as a one-liner. However, business is personal!

This has to be the main factor when working with someone – you have to get along, have the confidence in them and also know that you can sort out problems if something goes awry.

Once you have your shortlist of contractors you want to work with, you can then look at price. Far too many organisations say they want an all singing and all dancing organisation. All procurement procedures are "followed" right up until the price point comes into play and then it's almost as if everything else is dropped and just the cost is reviewed.

This is another **BUYER BEWARE** scenario in that you get what you pay for. It's like buying anything – you get different standards and different levels of service. You need to determine what you want before going out to market.

The asbestos industry is like any other in that you get bottom of the barrel prices right up to champagne prices, but with each end of the scale, you will receive a totally different experience.

What do you really want? Do you like contractual fighting over every little element because the business' margins are so tight that every little thing is an "extra"?

Or do you like being taken to the rugby every week on the client account knowing that ultimately you are paying for it?

Or maybe a middle of the road approach whereby you don't mind getting involved with contractual wranglings a little and knowing your call would be answered and issue sorted?

Once you've decided on your desired outcome, you can then bring cost in because ultimately to get more you will pay more.

What should you expect with asbestos removal?

Works with asbestos includes removal, repair or any disturbance of asbestos. It also includes anything that is ancillary to or supervising it.

Every asbestos removal job is different. Most work with asbestos should be completed by a Health and Safety Executive licensed contractor. However, there are works that can be undertaken by non-licensed contractors. The technical definition for licensable asbestos works is:

- Where worker exposure to asbestos is not sporadic and of low intensity; or

- Where the risk assessment cannot clearly demonstrate that the control limit (0.1 f/cm3 airborne fibres averaged over a four-hour period) will not be exceeded; or

- on asbestos coating (surface coatings that contain asbestos for fire protection, heat insulation or sound insulation but not including textured decorative coatings); or

- on asbestos insulation or AIB, where the risk assessment demonstrates that the work is not sporadic and of low intensity, the control limit will be exceeded, and it is not short duration work.

Short duration means the total time spent by all workers working with these materials does not exceed two hours in a seven-day period, including time spent setting up, cleaning and clearing up, and no one person works for more than one hour in a seven-day period.

To give you an idea, all works with loose fill asbestos, asbestos sprayed coatings, most works with asbestos insulation, removal of asbestos insulating board or millboard, removal of large quantities of asbestos debris would be deemed as licensed.

Licensed works are required to be notified to the local enforcing authority (either local HSE office, local Environmental Health office or Office of Rail Regulation depending on property type) 14 days before works start.

The notification gives the local authority time to assess the proposed works and allows them time to book in a time to inspect the site either before or during the work.

The contractor can apply for a shorter notification period, which is called a waiver or dispensation. This is the same process and is usually accompanied by a letter from the client requesting a "waiver" to the 14-day notification period.

A waiver is usually only granted in emergency situations where there is a serious risk to health. In our experience, waivers tend to set off alarms in the local office, which result in further investigations. Expect a visit to the site where there is a waiver, because if there's a risk to health it will need investigating.

Waivers are rarely granted for monetary reasons and definitely never for poor planning so beware in giving these reasons, as these will usually be investigated further. Where work on asbestos is not licensed, then non-licensed contractors may carry out the works. Although the contractor does not need a license, they still need to comply with the asbestos regulation and will need the following:

- All asbestos works must have suitable risk assessments to determine the potential risks.

- All contractors must have had suitable training (Non-licensed training specific to the type of material they're working with).

- Contractors must have appropriate Personal Protective Equipment and Respiratory Protective Equipment, which must have been suitably face fit tested for the user.

- Contractors must have appropriate equipment to complete the works (e.g., "Hepa filter" type vacuum cleaners), which must meet the required standards, hold routine maintenance certificates.

- If disposing of waste, contractors must be certified by the environment agency and have suitable vehicles for waste transit.

- Contractors should be suitably insured.

To give you an idea, works with asbestos cement, asbestos vinyl, asbestos textured coatings, asbestos resins, removal of very small amounts of asbestos debris would be deemed as non-licensed.

Some non-licensed works are notifiable (Notifiable Non-licensed).

Non-licensed works become notifiable if the material is friable or is degraded (poor condition/damaged) or would be degraded (broken up/damaged) as part of the removal.

The notification has to be submitted online before work begins. Contractors undertaking notifiable non-licensed works are required to have medicals every 3 years and their employers must maintain health records for them.

Works with asbestos enclosures – Fully Controlled

What is fully controlled conditions?

The term fully controlled is often used when describing the use of an asbestos enclosure.

Enclosures are used when undertaking licensed activities such as the removal of asbestos insulation or asbestos insulating board.

They involve the use of purpose built polythene structures, which surround and enclose the asbestos materials being worked on.

The enclosures are placed under negative pressure, which helps ensure that if there is a minor breach in the enclosure that air is drawn in rather than out.

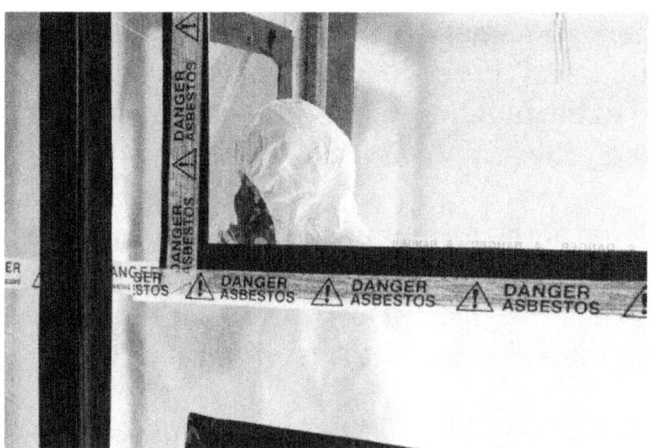

Access into the enclosure is either through purpose built airlocks or by a direct connection to a decontamination unit.

Decontamination units are required for all enclosure works. This comprises of dirty, shower and clean compartments and enables full decontamination of operatives.

Waste is removed from the enclosure usually via a purpose built waste lock.

As part of enclosure works whether it be removal or remedial. All dust and debris must be removed from the areas prior to the enclosure being dismantled.

All cleanable items must be cleaned and non-cleanable items must either be removed or sealed. Non-cleanable items may be items such as fibreglass insulation, fabrics, etc.

If it can't be wiped clean, then it potentially could be contaminated with asbestos fibre. Therefore, it needs to be removed or made safe.

You can expect damage to occur to the surrounding areas of the building. Where the polythene sheeting has been attached to the building, there will be tape marks, staple marks and general decorative damage.

All elements of the former enclosure should be completely removed as part of the dismantling process. If tape or sheeting remains, then the certificate of reoccupation has not been completed to a satisfactory standard.

Prior to the area being handed back to the occupants, the enclosure has to be independently checked to ensure it is free from all dust and debris. This process is called a four-stage clearance and results with issuing a certificate of reoccupation.

The process includes checks of the scope of the works, that the contractor plan of works is in line with what has been completed, visual examination of the enclosure, decontamination unit, waste routes/transit routes, air testing of the enclosure and a final examination of the former area once the enclosure is removed.

Works without enclosures – Suitably Controlled

What is suitably controlled conditions?

Where asbestos works are completed that do not require the use of an enclosure, they are completed under suitably controlled conditions. These works will be completed within an exclusion zone.
This is typically a barriered off area surrounding the work location, allowing a suitable minimum distance that the occupants can come to the asbestos area.

These areas should be suitably signed as respirator areas to prevent unauthorised access. The contractor will use primary decontamination facilities. This is usually in the form of a Hepa filter vacuum, buckets of clean water and sponges.

Again, all asbestos work materials should be removed post completion of the works. No independent check is required for these works. However, the contractor should self-certify that the works have been completed to a satisfactory standard.

Although it's not a requirement, we would always recommend that an independent check and air testing is completed as evidence that the former asbestos areas are safe to reoccupy.

CHAPTER BULLET POINTS

- Specification is key.
- Contractor competence is key.
- Various steps can be followed to check competence.
- Cost will vary depending on your desired outcome.
- Fully Controlled = enclosure, decontamination unit, independent certification.
- Suitably Controlled = exclusion zone, localised decontamination, contractor self-certify.

CHAPTER 11 Getting Stuff Done

Contractor Competency Checklist

All elements covered in this chapter have been turned into a form that can be downloaded and edited with your logo and data added.

Send this to the asbestos contractors to complete and ask them to send you copies of everything required.

Visit the following webpage to download a copy:

www.asbestosthedarkarts.com/asbestos-contractor-competence-check

Asbestos Contractor Competence Check

Page 1 is for you to request / carry out. Page 2 should be sent to the contractor to complete.

Contractor Name and Address
HSE Licence
Visit and check: https://webcommunities.hse.gov.uk/connect.ti/asbestos.licensing/view?objectId=8516
HSE Licence
Check there are no additional conditions on licence.
ISO Accreditation's
Request certificates
Insurance Cover
Check minimum policies required for the project. Ensure cover is to a decent amount vs risk – if an asbestos project goes wrong the figures can be astronomical!
ARCA / ACAD Member
Confirm member details and confirm the associations joining criteria
CHAS/Constructionline/Achilles/Exor
Confirm member details and confirm the joining criteria

CHAPTER 12

Asbestos Management Plans

The what, how, where and when

The asbestos management plan is the overarching document that details how you plan to manage asbestos.

Asbestos Management Plans in principle should be relatively easy and straightforward to put together - this, however, will depend on the complexity of asbestos at the site and the extent of the portfolio. The more complex set of asbestos and sites will equate to a more complex management plan.

Consideration will have to be made into how the site(s) are to be managed and any complications each site has.

For a large portfolio, this may require an overarching policy concerning the asbestos management policy with individual sites beneath having their own site plans. For instance, a multi-site factory will require a plan that covers each site as well as each operational unit on site e.g., the factory and warehouse will require different management principles to the offices.

Other factors will need to be considered such as visitor and contractor control - does everyone report into the same reception or do the different buildings have their own reception? If so, how will all these entry points be handled?

Something to remember:
Asbestos regulations are in place to stop people from being exposed to asbestos.

Every asbestos regulation is geared towards this simple principal.

As we touched on in the previous chapters, the greatest risk to people from asbestos these days is accidental disturbance. Which is why, as a building manager, you must ensure that the asbestos in your building is safe and being managed.

Dutyholders are required to ensure that a written plan to manage the asbestos risk is prepared. This can be in a paper or electronic format.

The asbestos management plan (AMP) should set out how the asbestos risks should be managed. Most importantly, whatever procedures are written about, they must be put into action. There's no point writing the best management plan in the world if you don't actually follow it. So be realistic and practical in your approach.

The approved code of practice states that the asbestos management plan should:

Identify the person or persons responsible for managing the asbestos risk;
(Who is the ultimate person in charge/responsible for the building? This needs to be identified and named within the document.)

Include a copy of the asbestos record or register and how to access it if it is kept electronically;
(It's not necessary to include the whole survey report. However, it must include the register, detail areas not

accessed and limitations in the information/inspections. The register must be kept live and up to date.)

Highlight instructions that any work on the fabric of the building cannot start without the relevant parts of the record/register being checked. The plan should include details for how this will be achieved.
(If you don't have a procedure in place to manage how works are undertaken within your building, then you urgently need one now. This procedure must include a process on identifying if asbestos is present. No works, which disturb the fabric of the building, should be commenced without first checking if asbestos is present. If you don't check, you have to presume it is present.)

Identify the procedures and arrangements to make sure:
- the record/register is checked in good time BEFORE the work starts;
(Get the areas surveyed before starting any works. How and who is going to manage/ensure this happens? How will you select the right company to complete these inspections for you?)

- checks will be made that the information on the presence of asbestos has been understood and will be taken into account;
(Make sure that all parties involved understand what asbestos information is available, that they actually understand what's present and what that means in relation to the works. Contractors will need to assess the risk of their works in relation to any asbestos present on your site.)

- checks will be made that the correct controls will be used and that competent asbestos-trained contractors will carry out the work;

(How will you ensure you appoint a competent contractor for any asbestos works? How will you ensure the works are completed to a satisfactory standard?)

Detail plans for any necessary work identified from the risk assessment, e.g., repair, protect or remove ACMs;
(Detail how you propose to ensure people are not exposed to asbestos fibre. Do the materials need to be repaired, removed, protected or simply have complete access to them restricted?)

Detail the schedule for monitoring the condition of any ACMs;
(Think about this carefully. Any identified or suspected asbestos materials must be inspected and their condition checked periodically to ensure there is no deterioration or damage.
The frequency of inspection will depend on the location of the asbestos and other factors, which could affect their condition. High-risk materials in high-risk areas will need constant monitoring. Compared to low-risk materials in low-risk areas, which may just need annual inspections.)

Explain how to communicate the content of the management plan;
(Think about how all this information is going to be communicated through your organisation and to anyone who needs to know it, which may be external parties. Training and monitoring will be the key to its success.)

Detail contingency arrangements if the main contact person for asbestos risk management is not available.
(What happens if you're not there – how does the asbestos management continue? Put the processes in place.)

Depending upon your site, this is going to be really easy or really difficult to put together.

A basic AMP may include:

- Who is responsible for managing asbestos (named dutyholder)
- Marked up plan of ACMs
- The asbestos register
- Assessments on the risk from asbestos
- Asbestos action plan for required remedial works
- Emergency procedures
- The reinspection regime for checking its condition
- Information communication plan for staff, maintenance workers and other contractors

A more complicated plan for larger sites and large portfolios may include:

- Asbestos action plan
- Asbestos management overview
- Contents
- Introduction
- Asbestos management principles
- Roles
- Responsible persons
- Policy and procedures
- Emergency procedures
- Intrusive asbestos surveys
- Planned site works
- Planned asbestos works
- Disposal of asbestos
- Information, instruction and training
- Material assessment information
- Priority assessment information
- Priority assessment risk definitions
- Material and priority data sheets
- Asbestos register
- Employee/maintenance staff confirmation records

- Contractor confirmation records
- Permits to work
- Staff training records
- Historical asbestos information and documents
- Management plan audits and revisions

Labelling asbestos

When asbestos in a good condition is present within a building, the recommended action is to manage it in place.

The process of how this is done should be fully detailed in the asbestos management plan as previously described. The management plan should detail how you plan to prevent the asbestos materials from being damaged or disturbed.

To aid this process, you may want to consider labelling the materials.

Labelling asbestos isn't a requirement of the regulations, but it is seen as a last line of defence in preventing disturbance of the asbestos materials.

We would have you consider that labelling asbestos is a good thing to do. In our experience, it really does help prevent tradespersons or occupants working in your building from disturbing the materials.

If someone goes to hang a picture on the wall (even though your procedures say they're not supposed to) and they see a big WARNING ASBESTOS sticker, they may think twice before hammering a nail into it.

So, what are your options?

The most commonly used asbestos label is this one.

The labels are approximately 5 cm (2 inches) in height so they're not very big. They do the job to a certain extent. However, they can easily not be seen on a large wall unless you place loads of them on it.

Our preferred label is this one.

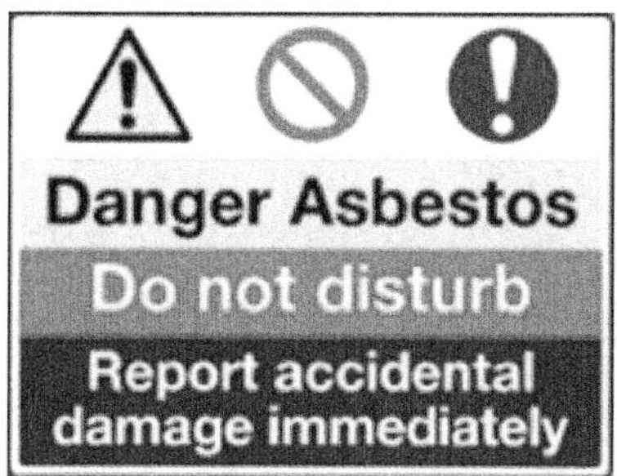

This is a tri-band asbestos warning label. The size of these starts at 10 cm (4 inches) but you can get these in any size you want. The three colours (yellow, red and blue) on the label makes it stand out and it is much easier to see when placed on a material. It also gives a clearer instruction to anyone that comes across it.

Depending on the type of building you have, labelling is not always ideal. You may not wish to advertise the fact that you have asbestos in your building.

For example, a restaurant may not wish to advertise the fact that there are asbestos materials in the building to its customers. In these circumstances, you may wish to create a discrete labelling method to complement your management system.

An option would be a tri-band label like this, which doesn't have the word asbestos on it.

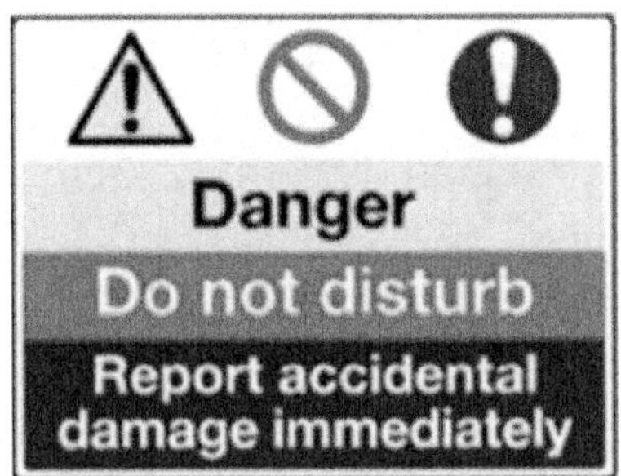

We have seen some clients use symbols like these to label their asbestos. Using these just needs a bit more caution and effort to communicate their meaning to the right people.

CHAPTER BULLET POINTS

- The asbestos management plan is the overarching document detailing how you will manage your asbestos.

- They should be simple to understand.

- They can be easy or difficult to put together depending on your asbestos and site complications.

- Consider labelling asbestos.

CHAPTER 12 Getting Stuff Done

Asbestos Management Plan Template

All elements covered in this chapter have been turned into a template that can be downloaded and edited with your logo and data added.

Visit the following webpage to download a copy:

www.asbestosthedarkarts.com/simple-management-plan

Insert Your Logo Here

Asbestos Management Plan

Delete and amend all sections as required:

Site Name and Address
Dutyholder
Contact Information
Site Responsible Person

Dutyholder Role and Responsibilities:

Site Responsible Person Role and Responsibilities:

CHAPTER 13

Asbestos Reinspections

How often and who can do them?

A reinspection is a visual inspection of the previously identified asbestos-containing materials.

It is not a new survey. It will not identify new asbestos and no samples are collected.

The reinspection is undertaken to check that the condition of the asbestos material has not deteriorated since it was last inspected. The period in between inspections can range up until 12 months but can also be shorter intervals. The Approved Code of Practice states:

As a minimum, the management plan, including records and drawings, should be reviewed every 12 months.

So, every twelve months as a minimum, the asbestos should be visually checked along with the management plan to ensure all is still working.

Things to consider:

Do the policies written a year ago still work?

Is the control of staff and visitors coming to the site working?

Have there been any incidents during the year?

As mentioned above, the period for some asbestos items may be shorter for a reinspection. Items that have a high-risk potential to release asbestos fibres in high-risk areas for becoming damaged will require more frequent checks.

However, if there is a high-risk material in a high-risk area, there is usually something that can be done. For example, it could possibly be over clad or even removed to lower the potential disturbance.

When nothing can be done, then more frequent checks should be put in place. This is essentially a risk assessment for what should be in line with as far as what is reasonably practicable. Once determined, any item requiring different inspection periods should be detailed in the action plan.

Who can reinspect?

An asbestos reinspection must be undertaken by a competent person.

The HSE defines a competent person as someone who has sufficient training and experience or knowledge and **other qualities!?**

It's not difficult to reinspect asbestos for signs of deterioration, but it would be recommended to have some training to prove a level has been ascertained before doing so.

You need to understand the signs and types of wear and tear that should be looked out for.

You will also need to have the ability to record your findings and update the register.

Usually, asbestos reinspection reports are issued with updated comments, plus any changes to the material's condition as well as updated photos showing the new condition.

This is possibly something that could be undertaken by an individual at a small site. However, if there are multi sites within the portfolio, then this can soon become impractical and tedious to complete.

CHAPTER BULLET POINTS

- A reinspection is not a survey.
- It should happen annually as a minimum.
- The management plan, including records and drawings, should also be reviewed and updated.

CHAPTER 14

Asbestos Awareness Training

What you need to know to keep you safe

Did you know asbestos awareness training should be given to all employees whose work could disturb the fabric of a building and expose them to asbestos? Asbestos awareness training should also be given to their supervisors or anyone who influences those works.

The approved code of practice specifically states that all those involved in refurbishment, maintenance and trades should have asbestos awareness training.

Workers such as:

- Demolition Workers
- Construction Workers
- General Maintenance Staff
- Electricians
- Plumbers
- Gas Fitters
- Painters and Decorators
- Joiners
- Shop Fitters
- Plasterers
- Roofers
- Heating And Ventilation Engineers

- Telecommunication Engineers
- Computer And Data Installers
- Fire and Burglar Alarm Installers
- Architects, Building Surveyors and other such professionals

Only workers who can prove that the buildings they only work in are free from asbestos are exempt from having this training.

There are many ways to get this training online or classroom based. We would personally always recommend classroom led, face-to-face training. In our experience, questions always come to the forefront of people's minds during their training and if you're in front of a real person, you can ask them and get the answer there and then.

What should asbestos awareness training teach you? It should teach you:

- What asbestos is
- Why asbestos was used
- **What products contain asbestos**
- **Where asbestos products were used**
- Why asbestos is hazardous

- What diseases and health effects are attributed to asbestos
- Who is at risk
- Basic asbestos management and overview on regulations
- **Emergency procedures**

We've highlighted the three points because they really are the most important points you should walk away with from the training.

You need to know what asbestos products are and where they were used so you don't disturb them.

In the event that something does go wrong, you need to know what to do in an emergency. There are ways to minimise exposure by simply following a few specific procedures.

Make sure you get the information to protect yourself.

How much does it cost?

The average cost for an "approved" asbestos awareness training course is around £65.

That's less than the average monthly "Sky TV" package.

As with most things these days, training and levels of competence should be maintained.

Although there is no requirement to complete an asbestos awareness training course every year, the asbestos guidance states that some form of refresher should be given. The sole purpose for any refresher should simply be to help prevent workers putting themselves or others at risk of being exposed to asbestos.

CHAPTER BULLET POINTS

- Every person who could come into contact with asbestos should have asbestos awareness training.
- Training should be given to all tradespersons.
- Recommend classroom-based training.
- Find out where asbestos is, what asbestos materials are, emergency procedures.

CHAPTER 15

Emergency Situations

What do you do when the worst happens?

Now with all the best planning, organisation and following of procedures there still may be a time when an emergency asbestos situation may occur.

Let's face it – when multiple humans are involved, things can go wrong. When these situations happen, it's important to know that there are steps that can be followed to minimise and control any exposure to asbestos.

1. Discovery of suspect asbestos materials, which haven't been highlighted on any previous survey/inspection.

Set the scene:

You've followed all of your management procedures. You've had a management survey of your property and spot refurbishment surveys inline where works are planned.

However, your contractor is about to start works in removing some walls too. Before he starts, he inspects the ceiling void above the walls to get an idea of the best way to bring them down. He's already checked the survey reports and no asbestos has been identified within these areas.

As he looks into the void, he sees a suspect panel attached to the wall above the suspended ceiling.

Emergency Procedure to follow:

Stop all works within the area.
(All works must cease within this area. This needs to be communicated to all persons working in the area. This is to stop anyone else from coming into contact or potentially disturbing it.)

The area should be sealed/closed off.
(Access to the area should be restricted to again prevent anyone else accidentally coming into contact and disturbing the suspect material.)

The Contractor must report the situation to the dutyholder and make them aware of the situation.
(The dutyholder needs to know what's happened, so they can make the necessary arrangements to deal with the situation.)

The material should be inspected and tested by a competent person *<insert company details of asbestos surveying company if appropriate.>*
(The suspect material needs to be sampled and tested to confirm if it is asbestos or not.)

Where necessary, appropriate action should be carried out prior to continuing work.
(If asbestos is identified, you may need to have the material removed, repaired or made safe. If the proposed works can be amended to avoid the asbestos, this may also be an option for you. Only once the asbestos risk has been dealt with

should works recommence. Further investigations into how this occurred should be made.)

2. **Damaging or disturbing known asbestos-containing materials.**

Set the scene:

All procedures have been put in place. However, someone working on your site puts a hammer through an asbestos insulating board wall.

Emergency Procedure to follow:

Stop all works within the area immediately.
(All works must cease within this area. This needs to be communicated to all persons working in the area. This is to stop anyone else coming into contact or potentially disturbing it.)

The area should be sealed/closed off and evacuated.
(Access to the area should be restricted to again prevent anyone else accidentally coming into contact and disturbing the suspect material.)

Leave all equipment, tools and belongings.
(Do not try and remove anything from the area as they may have become contaminated with asbestos fibre.)

Do not attempt to clean up the area.
(This may create a bigger asbestos problem.)

Remove any items of clothing that may be contaminated close to the area. Place items within plastic bags.
(Carefully remove clothing items, roll them inside out and place in plastic bags.)

The Contractor must report the situation to the dutyholder and make them aware of the situation.
(The dutyholder needs to know what's happened so they can make the necessary arrangements to deal with the situation.)

Asbestos made safe or removed before areas are reoccupied.
(Specialist contractors will be required to attend the site and make the area safe. Air monitoring may also be required to determine if the area is safe for reoccupation.

Record the incident, and keep health records for any person(s) thought to have been exposed.
(Wherever any person is exposed, records should be kept of that exposure for a minimum of 40 years.)

Undertake full investigation of the incident.
(A full investigation must be undertaken by you to identify the fail point within the procedures. The management plan and procedure must be updated to reflect your findings.)

CHAPTER BULLET POINTS

In an emergency, there are key actions you can take to minimise exposure to asbestos.

- Stop works.
- Evacuate the area.
- Don't go back in until safe to do so.
- Get a specialist contractor in where and when required.

CHAPTER 16

Additional Resources

Where can you find additional information about asbestos?

The following is a list of additional resource websites that can be visited for further reading and information.

There are all sorts here from the Health and Safety Executive to other government bodies, trade associations and independently run websites.

HSE (Health and Safety Executive)
www.hse.gov.uk/asbestos
Asbestos is the single greatest cause of work-related deaths in the UK. The HSE site provides health and safety advice and guidance so that those who may be exposed to asbestos at work know what to do to protect themselves and others. This site is the biggest source of asbestos information based in the UK on UK law. You will find information ranging from what is asbestos through to complete management of asbestos-containing materials. There is a news page that has informative articles.

Environment Agency
www.gov.uk/dispose-hazardous-waste
The Environment Agency is the enforcing authority in relation to disposing of asbestos waste. Their site contains detailed information on asbestos and asbestos waste.

ATAC (Asbestos Testing and Consultancy)

www.atac.org.uk

Asbestos Testing and Consultancy Association (ATAC). The association has been in operation for over 20 years, representing asbestos testing and consultancy specialists throughout the UK and overseas. The ATAC site is a good source for providing up-to-date information within the asbestos industry. The association has direct contact with relevant authority and government organisations.

ARCA (Asbestos Removal Contractors Association)

www.arca.org.uk

The Asbestos Removal Contractors Association (ARCA) is a UK-based asbestos removal trade association, representing the interests of asbestos removal contractors and associated asbestos businesses. The site provides a list of licensed asbestos removal contractors who have passed ARCA membership criteria. The ARCA site is a good source for providing up-to-date information within the asbestos industry. The association has direct contact with relevant authority and government organisations.

ACAD (Asbestos Control and Abatement Division)

acad.tica-acad.co.uk

ACAD is a UK-based trade association, who support and represent companies working throughout the asbestos industry. The site provides a list of licensed asbestos removal contractors who have passed ACAD membership criteria.

UKATA (UK Asbestos Training Association)

www.ukata.org.uk/asbestos-awareness

UKATA sets standards in asbestos training and ensures that its members meet those standards. Any organisation that allows builders or maintenance personnel onto their premises should ensure that they have evidence of asbestos awareness training. UKATA provides a quality standard for that training. When asbestos is to be worked upon deliberately, using a UKATA member to provide that training ensures that the training provider has the facilities, knowledge and experience to properly undertake that training.

RSPH (Royal Society for Public Health)

www.rsph.org.uk

The RSPH is an independent health education charity and the world's longest-established public health body. RSPH offers various asbestos specific qualifications.

BLF (British Lung Foundation)

www.blf.org.uk

The British Lung Foundation (BLF) is the only UK charity working for everyone affected by lung disease. They provide support for people affected by lung disease, which includes asbestos-related disease. The BLF works in a variety of ways, including funding world-class research, campaigning to bring about positive change in lung health and improving treatment, care and support for people affected by lung disease. There is some excellent information on this site on preventing lung disease including health tips.

Cancer Research UK

www.cancerresearchuk.org/about-cancer/mesothelioma/risks-causes

Cancer Research UK is the world's leading charity dedicated to beating cancer through research. Their groundbreaking work in finding new ways to prevent, diagnose and treat cancer has saved millions of lives. This site contains up-to-date information with regards to different types of cancer. From symptoms, diagnosis and treatment, to research and coping with cancer.

Asbestos Diseases UK

www.aduk.org.uk

ADUK provides help and support to both individuals and families affected by asbestos-related illness. The site gives information on the different types of asbestos disease. There is information on legal support, patient support and advice to sufferers.

IBAS (International Ban Asbestos Secretariat)

ibasecretariat.org

This site provides a wide range of information on the worldwide issues relating to asbestos. Its purpose is to achieve a global asbestos ban. There are pages of facts and stories relating to this worldwide problem. This site has some excellent information.

Asbestos Disease Awareness Organization

www.asbestosdiseaseawareness.org

Asbestos Disease Awareness Organization (ADAO) is based in the United States of America. ADAO seeks to give asbestos victims and concerned citizens a united voice to raise public awareness about the dangers of asbestos exposure. This site provides information and facts on the issues faced by asbestos victims within the USA.

UKAS (United Kingdom Accreditation Service)

www.ukas.com

The United Kingdom Accreditation Service is the sole national accreditation body recognised by government to assess, against internationally agreed standards, organisations that provide certification, testing, inspection and calibration services. Accreditation by UKAS demonstrates the competence, impartiality and performance capability of these evaluators. All companies that have obtained UKAS accreditation can be found listed on this site.

Asbestos in Schools (Original Site)

www.asbestosexposureschools.co.uk

The aim of this site is to inform parents, teachers and support staff about asbestos in schools. It gives guidance on how to improve the management of asbestos in schools. It aims to encourage openness in the UK Government's policy towards asbestos in schools.

Asbestos in Schools (New Site)

www.asbestosinschools.org.uk

This website examines the extent, type and condition of asbestos in schools and the risks to the occupants.

It has a record of asbestos incidents in schools and advises parents on checking their school is properly identifying and managing asbestos.

It gives referenced evidence that asbestos is present in most schools in the country, and in particular how there has been extensive use of the more dangerous materials in places vulnerable to damage.

Mavis Nye Foundation

www.mavisnyefoundation.com

The Mavis Nye Foundation was created to inspire victims of mesothelioma. The aim of the site is to give hope to fellow victims and show a light at the end of the tunnel. Mavis shares her journey and hopes to dispel some of the fear and myths.

ABOUT THE AUTHORS

Ian Stone

I've written a little bit about myself, so you can get to know who's behind the book. I'm married to my wonderful wife Sian and together we have an amazing little boy called Jaxon. He's the funniest kid that either of us know – he's forever making his own jokes up and makes us laugh. He's a veracious reader, and I'm really proud of him and his achievements so far.

I love all things motorcycle, especially the IOM TT and the Moto GP – what those riders do is amazing. I love to cook outside on barbecues or in wood-fired ovens and really enjoy socialising with friends and family especially in the summer.

The downside to all the fun bits that most people enjoy is that I'm an asbestos geek. I started in the asbestos industry in 2002 and have carried out all manner of jobs in the industry.

It's an affliction, as once you're in the asbestos industry it's rare that you leave, but I love it! I really enjoy assisting people to move from a place of headache to asbestos freedom.

I hold the Certificate of Competence in Asbestos and am a Fellow member of the Royal Society for Public Health. I also hold several proficiency module qualifications in asbestos and occupational hygiene. With these qualifications, you can be safe in the knowledge that the advice you receive is that of a proven expert.

My asbestos career has been slightly more eclectic than most, which has helped provide such an overview of the asbestos industry and issues surrounding asbestos management.

I am a qualified and competent surveyor, air analyst, bulk analyst and consultant who has worked within both UKAS and Non UKAS organisations.

As well as working on the asbestos consultancy side of the industry, I have also worked on the asbestos removal contracting side by helping a business obtain their 1-year and then 3-year asbestos removal licence.

For over three years, I left day-to-day practice to become the Manager of ATaC, the leading asbestos trade association for Asbestos Testing and Consulting businesses in the UK. During my time, I helped develop new asbestos industry qualifications through the RSPH (Royal Society for Public Health).

Whilst at ATaC, I also lobbied Parliament, working with the Asbestos in Schools steering group, which was at the time headed up by Michael Lees MBE. Michael was honoured by the Queen for the amazing work he had completed following the death of his wife 13 years previous from mesothelioma.

After working together for a number of years, I approached several MPs to write letters of support along with an application for Michael to be honoured. Michael was subsequently honoured with an MBE on the Queen's birthday honours list as a Campaigner and Founder of Asbestos in Schools Group for services to the Wellbeing of Children and Teachers.

I rejoined practice after ATaC and I am now a Director of Acorn Analytical Services, which is an asbestos consultancy that provides various UKAS accredited services. I assist with the running of the business as well as providing impartial and practical consultancy advice to businesses.

I also provide free asbestos school audits and action plans to help bring their asbestos management into line as efficiently as possible and to help remove their headache.

Direct from the author:

"There are three major points as to why I care so much about asbestos management.

"The most poignant came when I met Michael Lees. His work was truly inspiring after the massive loss he and his family suffered. His wife was a primary school teacher who shouldn't have ever been affected by asbestos.

"The second was my son being born in 2012 and the worries that being a father brings.

"The third was the news in 2018 that the fire fighters that helped during the World Trade Center collapse had now started to die from being exposed to asbestos and other noxious substances.

"It just brought it home that asbestos is still a massive issue in our modern world. Everyone remembers where they were when they heard the news of that tragedy. This happened not long before I started working in the asbestos industry and that's why it struck such a cord. It's shocking to think that exposures have happened and affected people during my career – it really brought it home to me.

"I truly want to assist people with their asbestos management so that everyone can go home to their family safely."

ABOUT THE AUTHORS

Neil Munro

I'm Neil. I thought you might like to find out a little bit about me. I'm 38 years old – wow, it's strange seeing that in writing, as in my head I still feel like I'm 19, although the grey hairs say something different. I'm lucky to be married to my best mate, Eleanor. We will be celebrating 10 years of marriage on 11th October 2018.

Together, we have been very fortunate to have two children, Reid who's 8 and Freya who's 5.

It's great having one of each – one minute, I can be playing *Minecraft* and the next, I'm putting clothes on one of the hundreds of dolls who seem to be taking over our home.

I love eating! Whether it's eating out, take-aways, BBQs or cooking at home, I love a good meal. Whenever I look at the menu, my first thoughts are always *what's the biggest thing on here?*

Now I know this is probably painting a bad picture of me, but, in fact, all the above is more of a treat and I take everything in moderation.

In fact, I have the most disciplined diet of anyone I know, much to the humour of my work mates. I like to keep myself fit, which does allow for some of those extra treats now and again.

I've been in the asbestos industry since 2003 and I can't get away from it. If I'm not working around asbestos, I'm reading articles about it, writing articles about it, training people about it... I've even got pictures of it on the walls in my house.

This passion of mine has given me the knowledge and experience to help clients whatever the asbestos situation may be.

I'm a fully qualified and competent asbestos surveyor, air monitoring analyst, bulk analyst, consultant and trainer. I have worked within a number of UKAS accredited, Non UKAS accredited and asbestos removal contractor organisations. This has given me invaluable experience within all areas of the asbestos industry.

I am a Fellow member of the RSPH and hold a multitude of proficiency certificates in asbestos inspection, testing and licensed asbestos removal management. I've been an asbestos trainer for many years.

During my time working for an asbestos removal contractor, I was actively involved and instrumental in the company achieving two major milestones. Firstly, was successfully gaining UKAS accreditation as an inspection body and secondly, was being granted a full HSE license to work with asbestos. As a new company, all quality manuals, risk assessments, controlled documents, procedural documents had to be produced, rolled out, verified and audited accordingly.

As the founding Director of Acorn Analytical Services Northampton office, I've had the pleasure of assisting a vast range of clients complete their asbestos projects, always on time, always within budget. I specialise in helping clients who have asbestos issues over multiple sites and complex operational activities.

I work with clients to not only ensure that they become asbestos compliant, but more importantly that they understand what they need to do.

Direct from the author:

"So why am I doing this? From what started as a job has now turned into a mission. A mission to educate clients about the dangers of asbestos and help them manage the risk.

"Asbestos kills, there's no doubt about it, the evidence is there and if you don't believe it, then you're very much mistaken. Asbestos kills over 5,000 people every year and those figures are only the recorded ones!
"Asbestos is everywhere. It's in our homes, work, schools, hospitals, churches, you name it. What really fascinates me is that we've known asbestos kills for ages, years even. In fact, centuries.

"Yet here we are in 2018 and asbestos is still a problem. Ok, we're no longer using it in this country and haven't been for over 18 years.

"The duty to manage has been around for 16 years, so why don't people comply with it or even know anything about it? How can a law that is in place to prevent people from dying not be known? It blows my mind and is the sole reason for me continuing in the asbestos industry and for writing this book.

"Managing asbestos is not sexy, but it's essential and doesn't have to be complicated. Get the knowledge, take action, protect lives."